STORIES
For all ages

This book gives expression
to the author's
extensive travel and membership
of a speakers club

Pat McCarthy

Pat McCarthy

Published by
Melalan Publications
22 Churchfield Terrace East, Churchfield, Cork,
Republic of Ireland.

ISBN No: 0-9549917-0-2

Printed by Litho Press,
Midleton, Co. Cork, Rep. of Ireland.
Tel: 00 353 21 4631401

Dedicated to my wife Mary
For all her encouragement in getting this book to print

Acknowledgements

I would like to thank Bill O'Callaghan and the staff of Litho Press in the production of this book.

Just Me

My introductory speech to Toastmasters International.

Asking a friend of mine if he had any hints that would help me over my first Toastmaster hurdle he told me.

"Take a good hold of the Lectern and don't let go until you feel the tension ease."

I was taken back a little by this advice. As you see up to this, I thought a Lectern was someone who assisted at church ceremonies, and wore a Soutan and Surplice. However he soon straightened me out on this, explaining the Lectern was the stand at the top of the room from where I would deliver my speech.

I am married to Mary and we have 8 children, 4 boys, 4 girls and 13 grandchildren. Unlike the last speaker I am a child of complete passion, being the eldest of seven. I can assure you being first in line, is the wrong end of the scale. The youngest is always king, or in our case queen, and is usually spoiled by the rest of the family. What annoyed me a lot was, that I was expected to set very high standards for the rest to follow. From the start my parents had wonderful plans for me. What parents haven't? Would I climb the dizzy heights of the political or commercial world? Or would I, by the grace of God become a priest, and convert at least the continent of Africa? After that, be ordained a bishop, and perhaps all going well be the first Irish Pope? In retrospect I can see what fine sentiments these were, but I, wanted to be a long distance truck driver. In this as you will see later, I surely realised my ambition.

After a stint with the nuns at St., Maries of the Isle where I received my first Holy Communion, I was given to the Christian Brothers, Sullivans Quay. The less said about this experience the better. Although I believe I wasn't entirely a fool, after a number of years at the hands of Small Dan, Skin the Goat, Lash La Rue and others, I discovered I wasn't a Scholar, a Hurler, a Footballer, a Singer or a Dancer. I was let know in no uncertain fashion that I was probably the most useless piece of flotsam that had ever attended this fine emporium of education. However despite all this, on the eve of inter school games I had to stand on the steps with the rest of the pupils, and give voice to the anthems which were supposed to egg on our team to victory the following day. It seemed I was doomed to anonymity. Never being anything more, than just a face in the crowd.

At the age of 12 I heard some of my classmates were leaving the Quay and going to the Crawford Tech. There they would learn all about trucks, cars, and other mechanically propelled vehicles. I thought to myself 'This is for me.' But! no such luck. My parents decided the School of Commerce, Morrisons Island was the place for me. At that time of my life parents were not to be disobeyed, or challenged on any decision that would affect ones future. Parents always knew best. Well they thought they did.

After passing the entrance exam I was accepted, and spent the next couple of years learning book keeping and commerce. I also learned a little more about girls, but unfortunately not enough to stay away from them. What I liked most was, that there was no corporal punishment. It rested entirely with oneself whether to succeed or not. I liked it here but could not get the driving out of my head. At 14 I learned to drive and at 17 I procured a driving licence, and did some driving on my fathers bread van. Apart from about four months laying mains around the city for the Cork Gas Co., I haven't worked at anything else only driving. At 18 I started with a poultry firm going out the country to collect Turkeys, Geese, Chickens, and Rabbits. I spent a season driving a combine harvester, and then drove for a sand and gravel firm. From there I moved to a tour coach company. After a season touring, I left and spent some time with C.I.E., on the buses and road freight. Went to Cardiff , South Wales got a job with that great employer of the Irish, George Wimpey & Co. and spent a couple of years driving artic trucks hauling machinery around England and Wales. On returning home, I got a job on the Cork Docks where I spent the next 25 years driving Cranes and forklifts, loading out and discharging shipping. Now you might say the wheel has gone the full circle and I'm back driving coaches again. With my present employer I have travelled

England, Scotland, Wales, France, Spain, Portugal, Switzerland, Italy, Holland, Austria, Belgium, Germany, and the Chech Republic.

At 70 although retired, I still get the odd call just for some local work, and Thank God I am still fit enough to it. Looking back over 53yrs of driving I sometimes wonder, having achieved my ambition of long distance driving, what would have happened if I had set my sights a little higher.

A Boyhood Journey

Nobody seemed to notice, or indeed nobody seemed to care as the boy rode tall in the saddle, down Anglesea Street, along Parnell Place and on down the Lower Road. The saddle being an old coarse sack tied with binder twine around the mares belly. It wasn't much protection from the mare's boney back, but it was the best he could do. Before leaving O'Neills stables on Quaker Road his mother lit the night-light to St. Philomena, and had given himself and the horse a liberal sprinkling of holy water for a safe journey. After all he was only eleven.

The boy clicked his tongue and with an encouraging "Giddy up Moll" and a slight tap of the ash plant the mare broke into a long loping stride. His trusty steed picked up its steps willingly as if knowing that when their destination was reached, a wonderful week of idleness lay before her. This was her reward for pulling its owners bread van around the countryside, doing an average of 40 miles per day for four days, and then two handy work days around the city.

Trotting on the heels of the horse was a little wired haired terrier named Peg, what could Peg a little terrier bitch be thinking of as she kept pace on that tarred surface. She ignored all the other traffic, and as they passed the Railway Station on the Lower Road the hissing sound of the train as it steamed impatiently in the station, didn't upset her one bit. It reminded the boy of one of those big brewery dray horses biting at the bit, and scraping the ground with its hooves, anxious to start its journey up under the tunnel, and on to Dublin.

The boy liked to think that Peg thought of summer evenings spent in the city dump hunting rats. Or of week ends when she would sit astride the crossbar of his old bike, and complete with polecat ferret and steel bar they would travel out the country to hunt for rabbits. Whatever she thought of, one thing was sure, she was always alert and ready to defend her companion at the slightest sign of danger.

Always a great source of pride to him was the beauty of his city and its hinterland. As he rode down the left bank of the river, the long line of tall Elms that grace the Marina on the opposite side always made his heart flutter. They stood there like giant river guardians swaying gently in the breeze.

Another landmark on his journey was Woodhill House. This fine mansion was a couple hundred of years old and was set back from the river amid spacious landscaped lawns and gardens. It was once the home of the Quaker, Cooper Penrose, at that time the High Sheriff of Cork and after whom Penrose Quay was named. The boys class teacher had told them that it had once housed the most beautiful tapestries and paintings, collected by Cooper Penrose during his many travels. The house was then known as the "Irish Vatican" now it is known as the Haunted House. Legend has it that the ghost of Sarah Curran lover of patriot Robert Emmet, now roams the place dressed all in white bemoaning her lost love. It is also said, that one night, on the word of an informer, the soldiers came to arrest Emmet, but he escaped and swam across the river to safety.

Passing Tivoli he looked with interest at the river dredger discharging its cargo of slurry into what was called the "Tivoli Scheme." It was said that some day this large area would be filled in, and an Industrial Estate developed on the site. Also due to this work, the flooding on this part of the road, between Fort William House – A beautiful Georgian residence – and Dunkathel Bridge would be eliminated. The boy wondered if the people who came up with these grand plans realised how much filling it needed. It must be well nigh impossible to fill this whole area entirely from the dredgings of the River Lee.

However, his job was to get this horse to Barnetstown, get a fresh horse back to Cork, and let the future of Cork Harbour to those a little more qualified than he.

On the left of this road stood some great big houses, each surrounded with a nice wooded area with some beautiful shrubs dotted here and there through out their spacious lawns. The houses were built by those known as the "Merchant Princes of Cork." The boy had heard a few tales of the wild parties that were held in some of these houses, where the food was sumptuous and the wine flowed freely. At the entrance to one of these places was a great stone edifice with two huge pillars joined at the top by a stone cross-member. Lying on top of this cross-member was the stone image of a Great Dane. A friend of his father visiting his home one evening had told the boy that this was a memorial to the dog that had saved his master from drowning in the nearby river. It was made from hewn Cork Limestone, and looked most impressive.

Travelling on towards Dunhathel he could see the great Georgian mansion, Dunkathel House. This was set high up on the hillside overlooking Lough Mahon and Blackrock Castle. The teacher had also told them about this house, it had been built around 1790 by a Cork merchant Abraham Morris. He promised that some day he would take the class on a visit there to see the 19th century decoration, the marbelised walls in the hallway, the beautiful blue sky and clouds ceiling, and other wonder's that this house held. He also hoped on that day he would get to hear some one of the present family play the old Immoff and Muckle barrel organ, which the teacher said is sometimes played for visitors. The boy looked forward to that.

After passing Dunkathel Bridge they entered the Vale of Glanmire. The lovely village of Glanmire situated on one bank of the River Glashboy, nestles itself comfortably into the side of the hill which slopes gently upward from its main street. In fact its only street. The village is dominated by the spire of the Protestant church which rises majestically above the trees and shrubs of the immediate area. Legend says that Mary, Joseph, and the child Jesus crossed here at one time and that's how the area got its name. The Gaelic name being Gleann Mhuire, or Marys Glen.

For the boy just beyond Glanmire was the best part of his journey, he loved this part of the road. Here the huge trees, Chestnut, Beech, Ash, Poplar, and the odd Oak almost shaded the road completely, and he felt a real closeness to nature. He had heard many stories about the goings on around the river here. Stories of men and hounds that hunted the otter up and down its banks, and the tales of Salmon poachers and the different methods they used to catch the great fish.

From Glanmire through Riverstown, and on to Sallybrook was a fairly well industrialised area. There was Punchs shoe polish factory, a furniture factory, a grain mill and store. At Sallybrook the Cork Firm "Ideal Weatherproofs" had a textile mill whose mill wheel was visible from the main road. On the other side could be seen the old buildings that was once a flax mill, and like the "Ideal Weatherproofs" mill its huge mill wheel was also visible from the main road. The chimney for this mill was about half a mile from the mill itself. The smoke and fumes were piped up the hillside to be released into the atmosphere through the smoke stack which stuck out like a giant finger from the top of the hill.

The hill was known as the Bleachyard Hill. It got its name from the fact that the products from the mill were laid out in the nearby fields to bleach under the summer sun

Leaving the main road at Anacartan Bridge the trio continued up a narrow country road well furnished with trees and bushes. On entering this road the boy slipped down from the horses back, and still holding the reins he walked slowly from one side to the other. On this sheltered stretch of road many birds had built their nests, and he loved to linger awhile to check the progress of each brood, always taking care never to hurt or frighten away any of the occupants. His favourite was where a robin had built its nest directly beneath that of a blackbird. He believed he was the only one in the world who knew where a two storey birds nest could be found.

Climbing up on the horse again they travelled down Transtown Hill across a stream, up Rathfelode, past the big fairy fort that gave the area its name, and down to his journeys end at Barnetstown. Here he released Moll and transferred the winkers and the sack on to another mare. He lingered for awhile, drank his bottle of milk, and ate his slice of bread and jam. He gave Peg the meaty bone he had brought for her, and when they had finished headed the ten miles back to Cork.

He whistled softly, and thought quietly to himself not of the journey ahead, but of greater journeys which he hoped he would some day take. First to see the wonders of his own country, places of historical and archaeological interest and places of great beauty like

Killarney, Gougane Barra, River Shannon, the Bog of Allen, the Burren of Clare, Connemara, and many other places he had heard of and read about. Many had been famous and became synonymous with the history of our fight for freedom. All these he hoped someday to visit, and then who knows, maybe spread his wings and visit faraway places, that now at any rate seemed full of mystique and adventure. But always he would hope that the door of home would be left slightly ajar, awaiting his safe return.

On reaching Quaker Road and O'Neills stables again he watered, fed, and stabled the mare. He walked up home where his mother showed her delight on his safe return. She lit another night light to St. Philomena to thank her for his safe return. His reward for the journey was two red sores on each side of his backside, which had to be duly treated with the zinc, boric, and starch powder.

He then had his supper, and soon after went straight to bed, to sleep the sleep of the exhausted.

Memories are made of this

Looking back I sometimes wonder what the people around Kildinan thought, when a bunch of city children were let loose among them for two months each summer. Born in Cork City and holidaying in a remote cottage on the side of a mountain slope at Prapp, Kildinan, the change for these kids was enormous.

To get to this cottage, one left the main road at the Pound Cross on the main Cork – Rathcormack road, and travelled up the narrowest and rockiest boreen you ever saw. You see our parents ever mindful of their charges well-being, decided that if war, pestilence, or worse ever hit our city, here was a place where all of us would be safe. They felt that if Ireland were ever invaded the enemy would never venture up here.

Despite its ruggedness, on entering this boreen one was immediately struck by its beauty and silence. This silence was sharpened and accentuated by some of the wonderous sounds of nature. The buzzing of the bees, The trilling of the birds and the sound of the little river, tumbling gently over a rocky and gravelly bed. One got the feeling of being embraced by something akin to the supernatural, or, maybe a little like Alice entering wonderland. On the right as one travelled up the boreen fields sloped gently upwards, with a line of trees, mostly Ash, forming a boundry between the fields and the boreen. In between the Ash here and there grew a number of wild Cherry trees. These Cherry trees bore an abundance of fruit in the late Summer as did the Blackberry briars and wild raspberrys, which also grew profusely on this side.

On the left side was a beautiful glade or meadow about sixty or eighty feet wide. This was filled with such an array of wild flowers – Daisies, Wild Iris, Dandelion, and many others. An Buachaillán Buí or Ragworth although classed as a weed did not look out of place here. The mingling of their perfumes gave this place an aroma all its own. It was a honey bee paradise, with never a shortage of nectar. Also here, two tall pines stripped of their branches were felled across the river to form a bridge. This led to a path that eventually came out on the main Glenville road. We used this path as a short cut to mass on Sundays. About half way up to the cottage one crossed the river by an old stone bridge, and from here to its source on the mountain, both banks were of the river were shrouded with Sallys.

Shortly after passing this bridge was the O'Mahony farmhouse and farmyard with its outhouses and haggard. With its ducks, geese, hens turkeys, two collie dogs, and stables for the horses. O'Mahonys had two heavy type work horses used for all the farm work, -- ploughing, harrowing, reaping, etc., and one beautiful roan mare used for pulling the back to back trap to mass on Sunday, or for travelling into Fermoy to do some shopping. Paddy O'Mahony took great pride in this high stepping animal, always decked out in shining livery of brasses and leather. She was a beauty to behold as she high stepped it along the road never once losing her rhythm, never breaking into a gallop.

For us city kids our yearly stay in the country was a great education. Each day was full of adventure. After getting over the initial stages of trampling corn, running wild in the hay fields, frightening cattle and sheep, and generally making a nuisance of ourselves, we settled down. We started to look around us and see if the country had something more than this to offer us.

We found that if we wanted to, we could make a few shillings by doing a little work. So we learned to thin turnips, mangolds, and other root crops. We learned how to turn hay and make it into cocks. We were taught how to make a súgán, this is a rope woven from the hay, to tie down these hay- cocks firmly so the high winds would not blow them away. We were shown how to follow the reaper and how to make sheaves of oats, barley, or wheat and later how to stook them and later still, how to stack them. We could milk cows, feed calves and chickens, we were shown how to collect eggs without breaking any, and learned how to find the place where some wayward hen would be laying out.

We were shown how to set snares to catch rabbits. When we travelled the mountain we learned to distinguish between the different tracks of rabbits, foxes, badgers, stoats and other wild creatures that roamed the mountainside. We knew where most species of birds nested but never interfered with their contents. In a small river that ran nearby, a tributary of the river Bride, we learned how to set baited hooks and leave them over night, hopefully to find a trout or two captured the following morning. In fact so interested were we in every thing around us that we became more adapted to country-living than many of those who had been born and reared in this environment, even to walking barefoot through the heather and gorse. We helped at harvest time when the sheaves of corn and oats were brought in from the fields to be made into ricks in the haggard behind the house to await threshing.

The day of the threshing was one of the biggest days on the farm calendar, second only to the day of the stations. I can still remember the awesome sight of the steam engine and threshing mill as it wound its way up the boreen spewing clouds of black smoke. Its shrill whistle which could be heard for miles around warning human and animal alike not to hinder its passage. Then it lumbered into the haggard and set up between the ricks to begin its task of separating grain from straw and chaff. The straw from the wheat and barley was used mostly as bedding for horses and cattle, and a lot of the good oaten straw was kept for winter feeding and thatching. Some of the chaff was used to renew mattress filling.

When it came to dinner time the mill was stopped but the engine was left running, as the steam had to kept at a certain pressure. All were then brought in to the kitchen and sat around a table capable of seating maybe twenty people. I can still see the plates piled high with home cured bacon and cabbage, and a huge willow-pattern plate in the middle of the table, heaped to overflowing with floury potatoes bursting in their jackets. There was no wine served at these gatherings. What they called a half – tierse of porter was already tapped and ready for serving and one had the choice of draught stout or butter- milk.

When the threshing finished the engine and mill were pulled out from the haggard and got ready to travel on to the next farm. If this was late in the evening then the two men following the machine were given accommodation for the night and continued on the following morning.

At that time there were few radios in the district. On the Sunday afternoons of big games such as, Munster Finals, Railway Cup games, or All Ireland Finals, the neighbours would gather at the

15

house where the one radio was. Each would be given a drop or a bottle of stout. They would spend the evening listening to Mícheál O'Heiher, who with his own unique style of commentary could make them feel that they were actually sitting in the stand in Croke Park watching the game.

On Sundays and Holydays we would walk the three miles to the village of Glenville to mass, and we never late either. But then this was another adventure for us and we never minded the walk.

We came here each summer during the war years. While we were here we were looked after by an old grandaunt of ours, we knew only as Auntie. She was a low sized stout kindly lady and she loved us kids to bits. She had been bred born and reared in one of the many laneways of the Marsh area of Cork. Despite her very urban upbringing she took to country living like a duck to water. As far as I can remember, Auntie just arrived one day at our home on Quaker Road with a few bits and pieces, all she had in this world, and lived with us until she died a number of years later.

How fortunate we were in having someone like her to be our carer or if you like our Nanny. She was so unselfish in her giving. I would say she influenced my life as much as my parents did. She showed a great knowledge of treating cuts, bruises, or any of the ailments that sometimes plague children in their younger years. She had enough love to cover everyone, with a little extra for the one who may have been in trouble with our parents over some misdemeanour.

How she loved that cottage and the time spent there. I think it gave her time to reflect, time to think about the past. But, most importantly to her, time to think about eternity, where she hoped to be reunited with her husband and daughter, whom I know she missed to heart-breaking point.

The cottage was kept impeccably clean by Auntie she took great pride in it. Like any other country housewife she learned to bake bastible cake, and got used to cooking on the open fire. The kitchen was the largest room and had a big open fireplace, complete with a crane and hooks to hang the pots from. It had a bellows on one side, which was worked by a wheel turned by hand. This fire was used for all cooking and was the only source of heating as well. The fuel, such as furze and turf was to be had in plentiful supply on the mountainside. We kids spent some time each week collecting this fuel, so our supply was never low.

Of course in this cottage we also had our very own cricket, and we would sit cross - legged each evening in front of the fire listening to its chirping. We imagined we could see it. We would try and imitate its chirping, and we would talk to it as one would talk to a dog or a cat. As the family name was McCarthy we decided we would call it "Macker". We would throw little crumbs of bastible cake and some raisins into to the fireplace, and were convinced that the cricket ate these during the night, as we could never find a trace of them in the morning. What a wonderful childish innocent time.

These were neighbourly people who lived around here, and were always on hand to help each other at the slightest sign of trouble. They were country folk who believed in Pishógs and Fairies. But when it came to the crunch they never let such things interfere with their own judgement, because, most of all they believed in God and trusted in Him explicitly.

When our holidays were over we returned to the city and back to school. It was indeed a sad time. Even though we had to some extent been a bit of a nuisance some of the time, everybody wished us well and hoped we would return again next year.

We did return for a number of years until other interests took our fancy, and each went his or her own road. Now after all the passing years when we all meet for some special family occasion someone is bound to bring up Kildinan and the cottage, and we are brought back to those far off days, when we as a family really lived.

Quaker Road

During the war, and for a number of years afterwards, a stranger walking up Quaker Road would never suspect what a hive of industry lay behind the façade of these ordinary looking homes. Many houses here -- although built on the side of the street -- had fairly large gardens to the rear, especially those on the right hand side coming up the road. Most grew their own vegetables, and a number kept pigs as well. One or two of these gardens were not used for anything, and grew wild. My father loved the garden. He loved to experiment with the different vegetables especially carrots and parsnips. He found that carrots and parsnips usually grew stodgy and very rarely grew straight. I remember one time he got a lot of cardboard tubes, dug a hole for each tube and then filled the tube with soil. He then planted a carrot or a parsnip seed in each tube and those few that did grow, unfortunately didn't grow straight down they just burst out through the tubes.

We lived in number 45 which is just half-way up on the right hand side, we had a very large garden which ran down to the backs of the Douglas Street houses. Here we grew onions, lettuce, carrots parsnips, cabbage, and potatoes. On each Monday evening after school I would pick a few dozen of each, load them into my box -car and next morning I would be down at the Coal Quay at 7.00 o'clock. I would line up my box-car with all the other market gardeners -- Who all had ponys and carts -- sell my produce to the dealers, and be back home to have some breakfast before going to school.

The money I'd make on these mornings wasn't pocket money, but went to help run the home. I was the eldest of seven, times were hard, and every little helped. Even though we were poor we were happy. You see everyone else around us didn't have a whole lot either.

In our back garden we kept hens and ducks, we had two rabbits, -- a white one and a black one -- we had two wire haired terriers and two polecat ferrets which we used for hunting. We also had a little pond for the ducks. Coming up to Christmas the goose would arrive, and that goose would paddle away with the ducks in sweet ignorance until Christmas week, when for her, the good life was terminated. She would be killed and got ready for the table. Liam Jones a man who worked down the road in O'Neills would come in, hang the goose off a rafter in the out house, and with one quick pull on the neck it would be all over. He was an expert at this.

We were a family who never had much money or style, but in those lean emergency years, Thank God we never went hungry. Our father was a great provider.

Our father who was a bread man had a country round. On a couple of days a week he would take in Riverstown, Upper Glanmire, Pigeon Hill, Knockraha, and surrounding district. On the other days he would travel Templemichael. Kildinan, Pound Cross, and Glenville. As well as selling bread, flour, and other groceries, he would also collect butter and eggs, and these he would sell the following day to the wholesale stores in the city. It was a way for making a few extra shillings. A lot of the houses he would call to would at that time be fairly isolated, so many would depend on him to bring the news of births, marriages, deaths, and any piece of local gossip that happened to be going the rounds.

He was a man who could never refuse anyone anything, especially when there was small children in the family. So some peoples bills would run a bit high with little hope of payment until maybe the harvest time, or hopefully the one who had emigrated might send something home, or when some stock would be sold. On one occasion a farmer with a big family confronted him and told him his wife wouldn't be taking any more goods as he had no way of paying for them just then. My father said,

"You can't let the children go hungry. I'm sure we can come to some arrangement."

After some more talk he offered my father two bonhams as payment, and my father accepted. From that day on, and for many years after we always kept pigs. When the two bonhams were fattened and sold to the factory he then bought a sow in young, and so the cycle began. When we had seven or eight ready for the factory, the sow would be ready to farrow again. To feed the pigs we went around the area to collect what we called "The Waste" This was scraps of leftovers from the other households. In our back yard we had a big empty oil drum, this had holes punchured all around the base and a metal grill place about 10 or 12 inches above the base. This was then filled with sawdust and set alight. When it was going full blast, a huge pot was placed on top filled with "The Waste" and the whole lot, scraps of Bread, Meat, Eggshells, Cabbage leaves, and whatever else might be available were all boiled up together and fed to the pigs. We also cut some Nettles and added those as well. There was no patent foods available at that time.

Bobby Tyner who lived across the road from us was the envy of all the bacon producer in the area. You see he had the contract every week to clear the leftover communion breads from the Reparation Convent on Windmill Road. So when his pigs went to Murphys they all wore halos.

The morning when our pigs' were due at the factory myself and my two brothers would be up with my father to drive them around the corner to Murphy's bacon factory on Evergreen Road. This turned out to be a bit of a circus. First we had to get the pigs from the back garden through the hallway of the house, out the front door and on to the street. This proved to be the easy part. We then had to drive them up Quaker Road as far as Timber Cross and turn them down Evergreen Road.

But it wasn't that simple. These were stubborn animals, and would take off in all directions. We soon learned that if you want a pig to turn left the best thing to do is, stand on its left side and drive it to the right. If you want it to go forward, grab hold of its tail and pull it backward with all your might. If you want it to go backward grab its tail and start pushing it forward. A pig will always go in the opposite direction to which you are driving it. Try it sometime! When we got near the factory two or three of the workers would come out and help us get them inside.

My brother and myself would then go back home, have some breakfast and go off to school. A little smelly perhaps, but happy that that job was over us for another while.

Another time a woman from near Riverstown ran up a fairly large bill with him, and every week she had some excuse as to why she couldn't pay it off. This excuse is probably the most original and funniest one she used. When my father arrived outside her door on Friday evening she came out and looked very distraught.

"Oh Mr Mac" She cried "I'm so sorry I haven't any money to give you off the bill. Mick had a terrible accident on his way home from work this evening, but Thank God he wasn't badly injured himself. He had a very narrow escape Mr Mac."

My father was shocked. And thinking that Mick was in a bad way asked Bridie.

"My God Bridie what happened? Was he knocked down by a car or a bus, or what?"

" No Mr. Mac, he might have been better off if he was. He was cycling down the Lower Road with his wages nice and safe in his coat pocket. Just as he was passing under the railway bridge the Youghal train was steaming overhead, the fireman was stoking the fire at the time, and didn't a spark from the engine fall right down into his pocket and set his wages on fire. A wonder to God Mr Mac he wasn't burned alive on top of his bike. Oh! Mr Mac the poor man he's inside now sipping a hot toddy trying to get over terrible shock of it all. So if you could just give me two loaves, a pound of butter, a pound of sugar, and a half pound of tea, I promise you I will clear it all off next week."

My father smiled and said "O.K." I think for entertainment value alone he thought it was worth chancing her for another week.

O'Neills on the left and at the bottom of the road – where the Telecom Building now stands – was a big poultry store. These people dealt in turkeys, geese, chickens, pigeons, goats and rabbits. They were very large market gardeners as well, and their plot ran along behind the Summerhill South houses and right out to Evergreen Road. They also stabled a number of horses here. O'Neills house was I believe the last thatched house in the city.

Each morning a lorry would leave O'Neills and spend the day travelling around West Cork or some other country district, collecting fowl and rabbits. In the evening it would return to O'Neills and discharge its cargo into the stores. At Christmas there would be much more activity when It would bring in large quantities of turkeys and geese. Women would be waiting to pluck the hens and other farmyard fowl, and we youngsters would be waiting to skin the rabbits. We were experts at this. We would cut open the belly, remove the entrails, pull the skin over the hind legs, give a little nip of a knife around the tail, pull the skin down along the body, over the head and remove head and skin in one operation. No matter how many we skinned whether it was ten or thirty, we would just get one shilling for our work. It was hard work and our hands would get rather raw and sore, but it was one of the ways we had for making a little pocket money.

Quaker Road got its name from the fact that a Quakers burial ground and meeting house are situated there. The entrance to the burial ground was once on Quaker Road but is now with some time on Summerhill South. The caretakers lodge is on Quaker Road and the people who lived there in my time -- Mr. & Mrs Johns -- were really good neighbours.

Oh! And by the way, has Quaker Road more words in its name than any road or street in Cork? Its Gaelic name is "Bothar Cumman na Gcarad" meaning "The Road of the Society of Friends."

On The Street Where I Lived

To look back isn't always easy, and some would say the past should be left in the past. But think again a lot can be pleasant to remember and maybe if we put our minds to it, a little profitable as well. This can be seen in the works of Alice Taylor who never stops looking back.

I got to thinking about this, and you know I was really surprised at what I could remember when I put my mind to it. Even the butter box, of which Alice Taylor spoke so fondly, was a major piece of furniture in our home. Apart from it being full of useless paraphernalia, it was my Fathers favourite seat. On this he would sit in front of the range, like the Tailor of Gougane Barra, after a hard days work, his stockinged feet inside the oven while he read the daily newspaper. Looking at him sitting there completely at ease, I always thought this must be as near to heaven as one could get in this world.

Incidents and people we took for granted, as just part of our community or our everyday life, were lost in the black hole of our mind. But now on looking back seem to come alive and stand out for their own uniqueness. On the street where I lived, Quaker Road, or in close proximity to it a number of these characters resided.

One that readily comes to mind is Jimmy. Jimmy was small and skinny and had a mania for hats or caps. Despite the fact that he had a mop of dark curly hair he rarely went around bareheaded. Like most of us youngsters of that time, during the Second World War, he came from a very poor family, and had a distinct appreciation of any scheme that would earn him a few coppers. He seemed to have a ready solution to most problems and was in his own way a very acute businessman. I suppose what we would call in modern day terms an entrepreneur.

He and I had our box cars. These were vehicles made from a timber box approximately four feet long by two feet wide, with an axle, two ball bearing wheels and a pair of wooden shafts. You see if it were wider than two feet, it would be very difficult to push or pull. With these box cars we would be out on hire after school to anyone who needed to shift furniture, rubbish, or whatever. But, our main business was the carting of turf.

At that time people in certain circumstances were issued with a voucher which entitled them to one bag of turf per week. We would collect the dockets from these people and for three pence per bag we would go to the turf store, collect the turf, and deliver it. In our box cars we could take four bags at the time, so on each trip we should make a shilling each. At that time a shilling was worth twelve pennies, now it's only worth five. However, some people would say they would pay us next week, so that would mean a loss of three pence. But! not for Jimmy. When he collected the docket the following week he would hold on to it until he was paid for the previous week. He left them with two choices pay up or freeze. I was a little more charitable and let the matter be, and so I never got paid by some.

Jimmy was also a great rhymer, and could for most situations trot out a rhyme off the top of his head. Like when old Mrs. Murphy who lived next door asked him to go to the local pub for a jug of porter. She gave him a very large jug, the price of the porter, and a half - penny for himself. Jimmy looked at the jug, looked at the half -penny, looked Mrs. Murphy straight in the eye and said "Mrs. Murphy the jug is big, and the money is small, so Jimmy's not going for your porter at all." And that was that. Negotiations were not entered into.

Today Jimmy is a big business man in our city, while I'm still only more or less a box car driver.

Another source of revenue for me at that time was Mr. Lucas our local barber who had his shop just around the corner from us on Douglas Street. He was a very flambuoyant character and his limitless knowledge of whatever subject happened to be under discussion in his shop, always amazed me.

His shop consisted of one room about twenty feet by twelve feet, with a wooden seat along one wall. It had two barbers chairs, two large mirrors, a leather strop for sharpening the razors, numerous ponnies, these were tin cups, in which he would mix the soap and hot water until he had a good lather to apply to the customers face. There was a very large sink, and three brass spittoons. The walls were covered with clippings from newspapers, photographs of great fighters such as, Jack Johnson, Steve Casey, known as Crusher Casey, Dan O'Mahony and many more. Some famous racehorses and their jockeys also hung there. I can only remember just two of the jockeys, Steve Donoghue, and Mickey Beery.

In between all of those was a notice that read,

"Please do not spit as it is both offence and dangerous."

Of course he was the worst offender himself. Every so often he would roll a big glougar of a spit around on his tongue and let it go in the direction of one of the spittoons, making it ring with a sound that would make Shandon green with envy.

Mr. Lucas also visited the South Infirmary hospital and would give a shave or a haircut to any patient who needed it. He never charged for this service. Relatives of men who died in hospital would call on Mr. Lucas and ask if he would shave the corpse. It was said that while he performed this task he would always sing that popular old song,

"Old pal why don't you answer me?"

Anyway getting back to Mr. Lucas as a source of revenue. When it was time for me to get a haircut, which would be around every three weeks, I would be at his shop at five past one on a Saturday. I would arrive just before the workmen would come in for their weekly shave. I had this timed to a T., to be there and take my place at the head of the queue as the first customer arrived. Mr. Lucas would then say to me "Mac would you ever give Mr. so and so a turn."

And I would always say "Of course Mr. Lucas."

This would go on for five or six men and when the backlog was cleared he would then cut my hair. When he finished I would slip down from the chair get my four pence from my pocket to pay him, and he would always say,

"Ah, that's alright Mac you've done those men a good turn."

So I had my hair cut and the price of the pictures in the evening all for the one four pence.

Another great lark for the pictures when money was scarce was, for us youngsters to make up four pence between us. One of us would go into the Palace Cinema on McCurtain Street and purchase a ticket. On gaining admission he would then make his way up to the gods and sneak down the back stairs, pull the bolt on the door that led on to Patricks Quay, leaving the rest of us in nice and quietly. After bolting the door again we made our way up to the gods. In this way five or six of us would have got in for the price of one ticket.

Somehow I always got a guilty feeling when the usher shone his torch in our direction he seemed to have a look of great suspicion on his face. But! I don't think he ever figured it out.

Beautiful City

Cork, a beautiful and friendly city is loved by natives and visitors alike. It was once known as the Venice of the west, this was due to the waterways which transversed it. These have since been covered over and are now our main thoroughfares. In Cork you have urban living with a definite rural atmosphere. It's like a village where everyone knows everyone, and no secret is safe. Just observe any day groups of people taking a little time out in Cafés, Shopping Malls, or on the sidewalks to talk and to gossip. There is no hurry, and no hustle and bustle that you find in other cities.

It was not always like this. There was a time when our city was drab, run down, and very badly neglected. Apathy seemed to reign everywhere. Nobody not even our municipal council, showed a whole lot of interest. They didn't seem to notice that the physical fabric of our city was crumbling around us, and that our streets and footpaths were virtually impassable. It was a city of blocked shores and gutters. When it rained it was bad enough putting up with the downpour, without trying to dodge the water cascading like Niagara Falls from overflowing blocked chutes. Then there were the loose slabs on our sidewalks squelching under ones feet, and with each squelch water would shoot up ones trousers as far as the knee. I often thought 'Thank goodness I don't wear a skirt.' At that time we also had our share of potholes, and when a car hit one of these all and sundry were sprayed with dirty water. As a matter of fact, thanks to its potholes Cork was once known as the "Holey City." Cattle lorries were allowed through our city at that time and would often spew slurry around the streets. They certainly added a definite hue to the overall drabness. Our river a virtual open sewer stank to high heaven and was definitely to be bypassed, especially at low tide during the Summer time.

Mind you even then we had a lot to be proud of. We had quite a number of buildings of beautiful architectural design. Many of which were built of our local quarried limestone and red sandstone.

Buildings like our City Hall, St. Anns Shandon, St. Marys, Popes Quay, our Courthouse, St. Finbarrs Cathedral, the School of Art, the Model School, now our second courthouse, and parts of Patrick

Street our main shopping area. A number were built from the red brick that was brought in as ballast on ships coming from England to pick up cargo here. But, we also had many eyesores.

Then came a great renaissance, our city fathers with their planners and architects seemed to suddenly become aware of our plight. They could be seen around town jotting down notes on all derelict areas. Noting where shrubs and bushes were growing out of some buildings, and a number with outcrops of near forests. With overgrown water chutes looking like neglected hanging baskets, and many of these buildings suffering from sheer carelessness.

When all the paperwork had been gone through and arranged in order of priority, the remedial work began, and what a change. Contractors were brought in. Eyesores were demolished, their innards consigned to the city dump, and new modern structures erected in their place.

Where once stood the old rat infested tenements rose modern apartment complexes. Where shored up buildings hung almost defying gravity, is now the inner city Bishop Lucey Park, with its beautiful wrought iron gates and limestone arches. These gates and arches once formed the entrance to the old Corn Exchange at Anglesea Street, later to be to be taken over by our corporation for storage, vehicle parking, and an administration depot.

Each limestone block was numbered and then the pillars and arches were carefully removed stone by stone, and re-erected at Bishop Lucey Park. Also within the park enclosure is part of the old city walls dating back to the 12th century, to Norman times. On the old site at Anglesea Street now stands our ultra modern Gárda Headquarters, our main Fire Station, a Multi Storey car park and also part of a modern highway.

Pedestrianisation of some of our city streets was also given priority. One may now stroll leisurely, or browse among the shops of the district that is known as the French Quarter. This is the area where the Huguenots after their suppression by France and Germany, settled in the late 17th and early 18th century. Stores and shops also took some renovation on board and good house -keeping is now the norm, out-side as well as inside. Of course the demolition of Merchants Quay and part of Parnell Place and the modern complex of a huge shopping mall with over forty different shops erected on this site, must surely be our flag ship development. Although built by private enterprise, Corkonians are really proud of it. It is a development second to none in this country.

The Firkin Crane – now home of the Cork Ballet Company – the old Butter Exchange, Shandon and the surrounding area have all taken on a new lease of life. Much of this is thanks to EU grants, and being designated an area where special tax concessions prevail. So inner city living is again coming into its own, and these areas have once more taken on the old human vibrancy of neighbourliness without the cramped tenement conditions.

Both channels of our river are now so clean, thanks to a new sewage system, that wildfowl are starting to winter here in the heart of the city. Also Salmon are finding it much easier to get to their spawning ground in the upper reaches of the river. And now with the building of a waste water treatment plant in the lower reaches of the harbour, we should see once again after many years swimmers taking to the water at Popes Quay.

2005 will see our City the "European Capital of Culture." In any language, a proud moment in our history. Just now it is taking on the mantle of a city bursting with energy and change. As one walks around our busy streets there is a vibrancy in the air, something one can't see, but can be felt, in body and soul. Patrick Street our main street, will be the envy of many other European Capitals, with its beautiful new paving and ultra modern lighting. Its trees and new pieces of sculpture enhancing its beauty further. All so captivating and pleasing to the eye of locals and visitors.

The program of events for 2005 is so varied, that we believe every taste will be more than catered for. Like 1991 the year of the Tall Ships, we are sure 2005 will be yet another year to remember. And the Annals of History will record for future generations that moment in time, when Cork was hailed as, and more than lived up to, the honour bestowed on it, the "European Capital of Culture."

We look forward to the future with a large degree of optimism. We hope that improvements to our city and its environs will continue, and that we will also see the demise of the Graffiti Artist and the Litter Lout, who still continue to scourge us with their dubious talents and thoughtlessness.

Kilroy is Alive and Well

Looking down from any of the slopes that surround our beautiful city makes me think, " Do we deserve the municipal leaders we have been blessed with over the years." We may not agree with some of the projects they have come up with to top up their finances etc., but we must agree, that they have, to the best of their ability, strove to beautify our city. With such schemes as Bishop Lucey Park, Peace Park, our pedestrianised areas, our beautiful riverside walks, and their input into the restoration of many fine buildings such as the Firkin Crane, the Butter Market and many more, must surely be appreciated. But the work of the Graffiti Artist is all too visible on most of these.

If one would only take the time to travel to any one of the vantage points around our city, one would be amazed at the amount of greenery to be seen when viewing from any one of these points. From the summit of Patricks Hill, Sundays Well, Montenotte, Gurranebraher, or Farmers Cross, the vistas laid out before us more than compare with any of those I've seen on visits to other cities at home or abroad. From each of these points unfolds a different panorama of beauty and life. Our river, approaching from the west through lush meadows and wooded glens divides our city North and South, while cradling its heart as it passes leisurely East on it's way to the sea.

Our Cathedrals, Churches, Civic Centre, Theatres, Galleries, and Cultural Centres, placed so strategically as if on some giant chess board to compliment and show off our many green areas. But, as Nancy Griffith sings, " From a distance the world is blue and green, and the snow-capped mountains white."

Come with me my friends, and see what the graffiti artist has done to vandalise the work of many of our city planners and architects. Men such as Philip Monaghan, Walter McEvelly, Joe Mchugh, Tom McNamara and our present city architect Neil Hegarty, to name just a few.

Our Civic Centre, our City Library, Churches, Banks, Public Buildings and even some Private Dwellings have been despoiled. They have all become victims of graffiti at some time or another. It seems nothing is sacred to the marker and spray can brigade. People tell me that the defacement of our city is a protest against the establishment, a way of getting a message across, a way of letting off steam. There are so many forms' of graffiti, that sometimes a stroll through our town can be quite upsetting. Some of it may be humorous, some of it may be downright vulgar and immoral, a lot is quite hurtful to individuals and indeed to groups and organisations also. Some is so sexually explicit with names and acts performed by certain individuals as to be criminal.

But, I think most will agree that whatever category it falls under, it is an eyesore and a visual assault on many peoples enjoyment of a lot of facilities, be they social, cultural, sporting, or otherwise. Mind you a lot of these are talented people. Not just some Joe Soap, or Moll Flops with a chip on his or her shoulder. This can be seen from some of the sketches and paintings that they produce to illustrate their point of view. I think a lot of it is a waste of good talent, and it is a pity that it cannot be chan-elled into more constructive and mind satisfying schemes.

A number of years ago a law was passed which forbade fly posting and which would also cover littering our streets. I have yet to see or hear of anyone being brought before the courts on any of these crimes against our city. Yet every day posters can be seen hanging from E.S.B. or P&T

poles, or stuck on generator light control housings.

You might say "What about some of our property owners?"
I will say "Yes indeed."

Take a walk with me along some of our finest thoroughfares, roads leading in and out of our city, and see the first and last view visitors have as they enter and leave our city. There are bushes and shrubs growing from derelict and not so derelict buildings. On several buildings on our side streets one may observe the outcrop of potential forests. Then there are the service companies who come along dig up our roads, move on to the next job, and leave behind the potholes.

To my mind these are also Graffiti Artists in their own right, although thankfully of late this practise is less prevalent than in former years.

Our Corporation has been accused from time to time of being perpetrators of Graffiti themselves, when they put in place those blue steel sculptures at Penrose Quay and Wilton Roundabout. Take a look at "Wake up Love" in Winthrop Street or the one entitled "City" on the South Mall. But I suppose "Beauty is in the eye of the beholder."

Then there's the hoarding that's put around some derelict building to try and hide the eyesore, this then becomes another canvas for the Graffiti Artist. Thus the cover up becomes more unsightly than that which it is supposed to hide. And of course graffiti breeds graffiti. A lot that is written begs an answer, or at least some comment.

Someone writes' "Jenny loves Mick"

Someone else follows with "So what?"

Then comes what in my opinion is a classic "My Mother made me a Lesbian"

And to follow that "If I buy her the wool will she make me one too?"

So from three little words scribbled furitively in the dark, the scene is set for the complete defacement of the property. When it comes to graffiti we are certainly not alone, every city I have visited all seem to be cursed by this form of vandalism. On a visit to Amsterdam recently I spotted a piece of graffiti on one of the canal walls, when translated it read "Brits out, Ireland for the Irish." I thought whatever about our M.E.Ps, our Graffiti Artists are certainly giving international coverage to out troubles.

However I must say, in case you may be under any misapprehension at this stage, I love Cork, even though Kilroy is alive and well and living a full life here. I was bred, born, and reared here. I love to climb its slopes, look down upon its beauty, and soak up its atmosphere, and then I often wonder why, I ever bother to travel, from my "Beautiful City my home by the Lee."

Kildinan Vale

Tranquil scenes laid out before me,
Beauty leaps from every nook,
Rolling slopes and drooping Willows,
Purple Heather and babbling Brook.
Cuckoo cooing in the distance,
Listen to that mocking sound,
Jackdaws cawing, Thrushes trilling,
Lambs are gambolling near a mound.
Sun is rising o'er the hillside,
Glistening dew on grasses green,
Air as pure as milk and honey,
Lord!!! It's the most beautiful
Morning I've ever seen.

Hyku

Falling from the sky,
Children make it into balls,
Snow can be such fun.

Winters end is near,
The first blooms peeping above,
The earth yields to spring.

A cold wind chills him,
Unemployed he walks the street,
Lord! Pity old Tom.

He stands alone and begs,
A McDonalds empty cup,
The tool of his trade.

Big Issues seller,
In the pouring rain she stands,
Ignored by all who pass.

Dog gone!

Dan, a great neighbour, a wonderful raconteur, a man of patients, a man whose integrity could never be questioned, a man no matter what the situation would never raise his voice, would never shout and rave about the policies or shortcomings of others. In fact you could say he was a pussycat. He and his family lived in a beautiful exclusive area of Silverspring, New Jersey. The houses here didn't have any walls or hedges around them, the lovely landscaped lawns sloped gently to the street. If any of his neighbours had trouble with blocked drains, leaky roofs, washers on taps, mowing the lawn or any other household jobs, Dan would make himself available and quickly sort out the trouble.

When one day a friend came to visit, Dan was pottering about in his little workshop in the back garden. When his friend saw all the different tools and gadgets in his workshop he asked Dan what he made with all this gear. Dan answered.

"Mostly good neighbours."

Then one evening it happened. On arriving home a party was in full swing next door, and his side of the street was full of parked cars. Being the man he was he didn't want to upset anybody, so he parked his car on the opposite side of the street, making sure he didn't block off any driveway. When he went in home he picked up the daily newspaper, and was relaxing before dinner in his favourite chair, when the phone rang.

"Hello"

"Mr. Potterman?"

"Yes"

"This is Mrs. Winkle across the street, you've come home just now and you've parked your car in front of my property. Please remove it."

And Dan trying not to lose his cool retorted.

" Mrs. Winkle every morning you let your dog out, he comes straight across the street and craps on my lawn. Listen carefully Mrs. Winkle , he sure better not crap there again." Andslammed down the phone.

Geraldo, the Randy Jinnet

A market gardener by trade Mick O'Laughln lived in Ballinlough on the outskirts of Cork. He prided himself on the good quality of his produce, and his produce was always in demand by the shopkeepers in the City. These would come to the open market on Cornmarket Street, better known as the Coal Kay, at 7.00am Tuesday, Thursday and Saturday mornings and purchase direct from the market gardeners. Micks mode of transport was, by Jinnet and cart. A Jinnet is a cross between a pony and a donkey, and these are usually very bad tempered animals. Mick's Jinnet whom he called Geraldo after a leader of a famous orchestra, was no different. Mick thought that the braying of the Jinnet sounded so musical he deserved to be named after some famous music person.

Micks next door neighbour had a beautiful Rhode Island Red Rooster. Each morning the rooster would fly up on the roof of the hen house to greet the sunrise, with a very loud "Cock-a-doodle-do" On hearing this, Geraldo would stick his head out of the stable door, and such a caterwauling you never heard in all your life. Of course for all within about _ mile radius that was the end of that nights' rest.

Each market morning when they left Ballinlough everything seemed O.K. with Geraldo, that is, until they came in sight of the Coal Kay. Then the braying started. When he saw the other ponys and donkeys a discord of sound erupted from Geraldo as he headed for the street. However Mick kept him on a tight rein, and to try and quieten him he would start shouting and bawling almost as loud as Geraldo. Then along with the braying Geraldo also got a bad attack of flatulence, so with the braying and the blowing a cacophony of sound accompanied them as Mick steered him into position.

Unlike the other traders who backed their carts into the kerb, Mick always faced Geraldo in and put on his nose bag. However this morning it wasn't the wall of a building that was in front of him but the big plate glass window of a hardware shop, and Mick had forgotten Geraldos nose bag. Mick went to the back of the cart to deal with his customers. At this stage Geraldo looking at his reflection in the window really became agitated and stressed. He pawed the ground with his hooves for a short while, and then with one mighty thrust leaped straight through the window, cart, vegetables and all. A silence fell over the whole street as everyone stopped to look in the direction of the crash. Mick O'Loughlin could not believe his eyes as he took in the scene of devastation. Geraldo was in a heap inside the store, the cart and vegetables in a heap outside. The traces having broken, the cart rolled back on to the roadway again.

When Geraldo was eventually extricated from the mess of pots, pans, paints, brushes, ladders, and all kinds of hardware, he was indeed a very subdued Jinnet. Mick was arguing with the store manager about who was going to pay for the damage. Mick contended that he could not be held responsible. He maintained that any one with any bit of sense could clearly see that Geraldo, seeing his own reflection in the window of the store got so very randy, and like Narcissus when he looked into the well, he fell in love with his own image.

After that, Mick decided it was time to change to a nice quiet pony. Although he hated to part with Geraldo he left him go to a small farmer back in West Cork, who felt that with an animal like Geraldo he would at last be able to "Plough the rocks of bawn."

Cork Airport

It's got fountains and goldfish and birds on the wing,
It's even got a statue of the bould Christy Ring.

Jack Charlton sits by the pool with a smile,
Delighted to be back in the Emerald Isle,
Not football this time, but fishing I'll be,
It's great to be back on the banks of the Lee.

Planes are coming, and planes are going,
It's a busy place there's no denying,
People arriving from poles apart,
It may be small but it's got a big heart.

Now of late the push is on,
To make its heart more big and strong,
It's almost ready and it's rarin' to go,
And we'll be happy to greet you in Érin go Bráth.

The Poacher

Last Wednesday in our staff canteen,
Mick O'Halloran said that he had seen,
The finest Teelvision set, that he could ever hope to get,
For only 70 quid said he, "I'll have R.T.E., and B.B.C.,
I'll see Tolka Row, and also, and Dallas,
And watch the 'Pool beat Crystal Palace,
Boy you'd want to see the colour,
I'm sure a very lucky feller."
But sitting there with just a trace, of a sly smile upon his face,
And then the smile changed to a grin,
As Christy started to take it in,
He stood up, put on his cap, and said "I'm going for a crap,"
But crapping Christy never went,
He went the quay with bad intent,
Then went on board the "Carrigrennan,"
And met the mate called Mr. Brennan.
He said "I want that Television,"
And snapped it up with quick precision,
Then down the gangway with the loot,
And put it into Crowleys boot,
Who sped away quiet as a mouse,
And landed it in Christys House.
Now the moral of the story is,
That if you want a Televis,
Make sure that Christy's not about,
And if he is, just shut your mouth.

A Personal Anthology

Helen.
Though not from Troy,
is a lover of ships.

Pamela.
Her skirt was short,
But, not as short as her temper.

Liz.
Trudging on after her eight failure,
Is there anyone out there for Elizabeth Taylor.

Pauline.
A Lady endowed with so much knowledge,
I'd say, she probably went to college.

Pauline.
She sends out the proper vibes ,
To all of us aspiring scribes.

Pauline.
[Advice to writers.]
When an idea comes that's really good,
Jot it down.

Photographic Truth.
Why does it make us stop and stare,
Because the camera sees us as we are.

Tongue in Cheek.
We held up the traffic on the way to the kingdom,
Because nine of us were travelling in condom.

Sad Reflection.

Don't look too long in the mirror,
It may damage your ego.

Legal Advice.   [Free]
Keep away from those who in court wear wigs,
Or you may end up with bars on your digs.

Seeing the light.
Tripping the light fantastic,
Could blow your fuse.

Cork Airport.
It's got fountains, and goldfish and birds on the wing,
And also a statue of the bould Christy Ring.

The Wino.
Inside he screams, unheard, unseen,
And thinks of, what might have been.

The Addict King.
[With apologies to Shakespeare.]
A fix, A fix,
My Kingdom for a fix.

A Winter Anthology

Cruel Nature.
Winds and gales,
And stranded Whales.

Seasonal Complaints.
Sleet and wind and freezing rains,
Lord it's time again for those cursed chilblains.

Paradise Lost.
People pass the beggar and his old hag,
As they suck their sustenance from a brown paper bag.

Paradise Lost. [2]
On Patricks Bridge it's a tough oul' station,
God, but I'm looking forward to cremation.

Animal Crackers.
Birds, Dogs and Cats, leave their tracks in the snow,
But we're happy smooching under the Mistletoe.

From beneath the sheets.
Icy patterns on window panes,
Let's snuggle a little longer.

Carol Singers' plight.
Christmas carols and seasonal songs,
Won't keep you warm without long – johns.

Cheers
There's midnight mass and Christmas carol,
But, for most of us it's roll out the barrel.

Epitaph for our Minister of Finance

A lover of the filthy lucre,
He always made us sick,
As our wallets and pockets he'd pick,
Like the dog that went down with the mange,
He made us feel we had no future,
So he never returned our change.

Epitaph for our Minister of Agriculture

He was a bit of a clown,
T.B. eradication was his pet
But he never got on with the Vet,
Who with a great deal of zest,
Had the whole herd put down,
And that was the end of that pest. [The Minister]

Epitaph for our Minister of The environment

A man who knew every pothole,
Planted trees, flowers, and shrubs,
Around streets, houses, and pubs,
And the dogs of the street didn't miss,
And the trees and plants took its toll,
As on them they just had to piss.

Epitaph for our Minister of Justice

He wasn't a king among men,
Put them all behind bars,
For stealing money and cars,
When he had them inside,
With one stroke of his pen,
Said "Here for the rest of your lives you'll reside."

A Promise Kept

Minnie got up from the chair, put the book she had been reading on the book - shelf, looked at the dying embers in the grate, gave them a stir with the poker, and placed the fireguard in position. She then went to check the doors front and rear, and made sure each was locked for the night.

She then phoned the local Gárda station and checked her security bleeper to make sure it was working. From the bottom of the stairs she switched on the upstairs landing light, and put out the lights downstairs. Before climbing the stairs to her bedroom Minnie looked 'round at the room and became very aware of it's emptiness. Although it was filled with memorabilia of years gone-bye, these were but dead inanimate things and only served to provoke memories of days when this house was filled with the sounds of young people their laughter and their tears.

Now 48 years, 4 children, and 8 grandchildren later she was back to square one. She was even further back than square one, as she was now all alone since himself passed on almost 4 years ago. Often she would sit and think of those lost times. Times of happiness and sorrow, of great expectations and anticipation, when the ups and downs of family life were measured by the success or failure of some member of the family to fulfil their ambitions, or come back to full health after a particularly bad illness.

Tonight the atmosphere of the room was different. There was an assuring calm about it, like the calm that follows a storm, not visible yet quite tangible. Even the dog and the cat though each had their own separate corners, snuggled together near the fireplace tonight. All was silent, yet it was a kind of a vibrant silence. A silence though calming to the spirit, could, she thought, shake the very foundations of the house.

Bills picture on the mantelpiece smiled down on her in the glow of the Sacred Heart lamp. He was a good man, they had been happy together, and had always provided well for his family. A carpenter by trade he was never short of work. Sure wasn't there bits and pieces of furniture made by him in almost every house in the parish.

He liked a few pints on Saturday night and after mass on Sunday morning. Probably his only fault was that he smoked too much, and it was the cigarettes that got him in the end. She remembered how sometimes he would leave the kitchen gasping for breath, and go out into the cold night air to try and relieve his aching lungs. When he returned inside again the first thing he did was to light another cigarette.

Bill was forever giving up the fags, tomorrow, but tomorrow never came. She often wondered what was in cigarettes that made people so dependent on them. There were days when he could go through two or three packs. Although he never smoked in bed, he made sure a pack and a lighter were on the bedside locker each night before he settled down.

They had met at the local platform dance one Sunday night, had a few dances together, and then asked if he could see her home. Although they lived only a few fields from each other it wasn't until that Sunday night that they had spoken. It had taken up from there, and they married three years later.

Life was good to them and they had four children, three girls and one boy. Liam was the youngest of the four and was spoiled rotten by his three sisters, and each, as they say in the country, had married well. Though none had emigrated and they lived only about 40 miles from her in the city, it was seldom she saw them. She got the odd phone call but the only visit she was sure of was the one at Christmas. It was always a flying visit, none of them ever stayed overnight although she had plenty of room. Minnie didn't think that it was good for the grandchildren to be growing up barely knowing who their grandmother was. It was funny they themselves when they were growing up loved to visit their grandparents, but their own children hardly knew she existed. She supposed that the pace of the world had quickened some, and people didn't put the same effort in to keeping in touch.

Her mother once told her

"Minnie, treasure your neighbours, you may not always have your family, but, your neighbours will be always right next door."

These indeed turned out to be very prophetic words. She had wonderful neighbours. Some dropped in every day, others popped in at weekends to see if she wanted anything from the supermarket, and the man from the Meals on Wheels arrived every day at 1.00 o'clock sharp. All in all they were very attentive to her.

Bill loved the grandchildren too and his face lit up at their arrival, but he always complained that their visits weren't long enough, and often enough. He loved them and he felt that these would be the ones to see him out on his last journey. He had said to Minnie on a number occasions,

"Isn't it grand all the same Minnie that when our time is up we won't die alone."

It was at the time a very comforting thought, but where was everyone now if the Lord took it into his head to come for her tonight. There was a strangeness about tonight something she couldn't put her finger on, like a presence that wasn't usually there. She wasn't frightened, it was friendly and made her feel she was no longer alone.

Minnie took one last look around the room and her eyes went to the mantelpiece to Bills picture. 'My God are my eyes deceiving me?'

That smile on Bills face looked much broader, and there that wink, she was sure he winked. When Bill winked there was always something going to happen, it was a kind of a secret sign to her that he knew more than he was letting on. She smiled winked back and turned to climb the stairs to go to bed.

In the bedroom she changed into her night clothes, knelt and said her prayers. Tonight she would say her rosary in bed. Before getting into bed she put out the light and drew back the curtains. The moon shone in and lit up the room with a pleasant glow. Minnie got into bed, took her beads from the top of the locker and started to pray the rosary. On the second Glorious Mystery "The Ascension of Jesus into Heaven" a movement at the end of the bed caught her attention. There was a figure standing there.

"Bill? Is that you Bill?"

"Yes Minnie this is Bill," and stretching out his hand he said "Come with me, didn't I promise you, you wouldn't die alone."

A Mid-Winter Nights Dream

Catherine Bailey shook the rain from her umbrella, opened the front door of her two up, two down home and placed the umbrella in the brass holder just inside the door. She hung her coat on the hall-stand, and the holiday brochures she had collected on the way home she placed on the kitchen table. She removed the pre-cooked dinner from the fridge and put it into the micro- wave. While waiting for it to heat she put a match to the already set fire, and then prepared the table for her evening meal. When she had finished eating she cleared the table, washed the delph, and relaxed in her favourite chair near the fire.

It's winter again, the time for wishing and dreaming. Each year brings the same wish and that is, to visit and ski the slopes of the Shilthorn Alpine Mountain of Switzerland. Never being able to afford such a trip, all Catherine could do was to gaze longingly at the beautiful holiday brochures which at this time of the year she collected religiously. She hoped that some day, some how, some miracle would allow her to fulfil her life long aspiration. She had read so much about the Jungfrau region -- Jungfrau meaning young woman – where the Shilthorn was located that she felt she knew every slope, every curve, every jagged outcrop of this great mountain so loved by skiers and visitors alike. After going through the brochures again, Catherine sat sipping her night cap – a glass of warm milk – and felt a little euphoric. She felt somehow that this winter her lifetime wish would be realised. Just how she did not know, as money was not all that plentiful. As she climbed the stairs to bed she held the vision of that beautiful mountain in her mind. Snuggling comfortably beneath the continental quilt she gave licence to her imagination, and let her mind run amok. Hoping that if only in her dreaming, she could fulfil her lifes ambition.

Sleep doesn't come easily to Catherine as she tries to control her tormented thoughts. Eventually she succeeds. As she drifts into a relaxed void, below her she sees the lights of Zurich, Switzerland, and the aircraft descends smoothly to the tarmac. Quickly disembarking, and getting through immigration and customs, she makes her way to the coach park to board the bus that will take to the beautiful lake side city of Luzern, where she will overnight. Driving on next morning they head for the town of Interlacken, with a comfort and lunch stop on the journey at the little village of Glessenbach. After this very pleasant interlude they continue their journey to their final destination the little town of Interlacken.

Interlacken, -- whose name means "Between the Lakes" -- is situated between Lake Brienz and Lake Thun, near the base of the famous Mount Eiger. It is a town of great beauty, with most of its hotels, shops, and houses built in the unique Swiss style of verandas and crafted timber work. Her hotel is set against a backdrop of snow capped mountains, and the nearby lakes with their tourist ferries and pleasure craft look magnificent, shimmering in the evening sun.

After dinner Catherine takes a stroll around the town and finds the cold sharp air most invigorating. But, one must exercise a good degree of caution, as the sidewalks are fairly slippery due to the hard frozen crust that has formed over the snow. Then, back to the hotel to relax with a drink in front of a roaring log fire before retiring for the night.

Up next morning for breakfast at 6.00am, and then to be fitted out with ski gear. This consisted of an all in one waterproof suit, cap, gloves, goggles, skis, and those special calf length boots that can be clipped on to the skis. Then, with other guests from the hotel she boards the bus that will take them up the Lauterbrunnen Valley to the cable car terminal. On the journey upwards travelling between the mountains one can see where the waterfalls have been caught in their tumbling and frozen solid. They look like giant curtains draped over the mountainside. Lauterbrunnen, which means "Loud Water" takes its name from these frozen waterfalls. When the icicles break off in the spring thaw they cause a loud explosion to echo through the valley, -- Hence the name "Loud Water."

About four miles above the town Catherine leaves the bus and boards one of the cable cars which will take her to first level of the 10,000ft high Shilthorn. The climb is scary and the cabin is swinging to and fro in the wind and makes her feel a bit nauseous, but one is well compensated for this with fantastic views of snow covered slopes and wooded valleys. Arriving at the first level she leaves the cable car and takes a quick look around the little hamlet of Murren, whose houses are almost hidden by the snow, then she boards another car for the next stage of the journey.

To get to the summit of the Shilthorn one has to board four different cable cars, and for the last stage Catherine is delighted to see that the one she is boarding carries the logo 007. This takes her to the Summit. From up here the panorama of mountains, lakes, and cloud formations is breath taking, and so, between the scenery and the rarefied air Catherine finds it hard to breathe for awhile. She walks towards the restaurant, which is called "Piz Gloria" meaning Glorias Peak. She can't believe she is going to have lunch in this revolving restaurant located here on top of the world. This restaurant revolves slowly and by the time one finishes lunch one has had a complete view of hundreds of square miles of mountains, lakes, and wooded valleys. It was used in the 1968 James Bond film "On her Majestys Service" and on each of its windows is the logo 007.

A short time after lunch Catherine leaves the restaurant, goes to the ledge where she will start her downward journey, and straps on her skis. For a moment she hesitates and takes in all before her. Mountains, hamlets, lakes, wooded valleys and away in the distance floating leisurely among all this grandeur are a number of multi - coloured hot air balloons. This unique scene is what Catherine wants to take home with her, and plants it indelibly in her mind.

A gentle push and she's on her way. What a feeling to be gliding down the snowy slopes of Shilthorn, the wind like a freight train screaming past. Skiing comes so naturally to her that she feels quite amazed as she weaves and bobs on her way down, everything just a blur. On reaching the end of the run Catherine removes her skis and rests awhile, the adrenaline pumping through her veins giving her such a high feeling. She finds herself crying with happiness, it had been everything she had imagined it to be, and more. Boarding the cable car for the short journey back to the bus park, she finds it difficult to believe that her lifetime dream has come true.

Standing on the ski bus that will take her back to her hotel in Interlacken she gazes at the steep walls of the mountains on both sides of the road and once again admires their snow caps and frozen waterfalls. She feels so relaxed and unbelievably happy when a familiar sound interrupts her thoughts. It is her alarm clock. So suddenly is she awakened that it is some time before she can comprehend the swift location switch, and that she is really lying in her own bed. Has it all been just a dream? But if so, what a dream. No! No! No! it wasn't a dream, it was too real to think that she had just dreamt it, she tried to persuade herself.

Getting out of bed she looks out through the curtains of her bedroom window at the early morning drizzle. Reality is staring Catherine straight in the face. For a moment she feels like bursting into tears, but hesitates and feels that nothing and no one can take last night from her. She will hold it forever in her heart.

Catherine must now shower, have breakfast, and get off to work, and face the humdrum existence of her everyday life. But, never mind, she will always believe that she has been to Shilthorn and skied down its magnificent slopes. Deep in her heart she feels she's been there, done that, and all she needs to prove is the Tee Shirt, and she's going to get one somewhere before this day is out.

Sarahs Big Day

The sun shone brilliantly. A beautiful morning for a beautiful occasion. It was Sarahs wedding day and she, like the sun, gave out an aura of brilliance. She was a high society girl who was about to marry into money. She would marry James McConville, a self-made millionaire. Although coming from humble beginnings, which Sarah rarely acknowledged publicly, he had worked arduously to get where he was today. James, the owner of two night clubs and three off licence outlets, would be well able to keep Sarah in the manner she had always been accustomed to.

Being the only daughter of the M.D., of a top Stevedoring Company, Sarah had been spoiled and indulged in by her parents all her life. Her mother, a stunningly beautiful woman, also came from a very rich merchant family. Sarah had inherited her mothers' good looks and love of the good life.

Secretly Sarah hoped James would never write a book like that Dublin fellow who wrote "Little Green apples." Or "Penny apples" or something like that. Detailing his life from apple seller to millionaire. This would not be Sarahs kettle of fish. She always gave her friends the impression that James also came from a wealthy family. Although she loved James very much, one had appearances to keep up, and as far as she was concerned all skeletons were to be locked safely away in some forgotten wardrobe. Perhaps some would find his story fascinating. The fact that his mother sold second hand clothes from a stall on the Coal Quay, and that his father who had passed away a couple of years ago, worked on the Cork Docks for her fathers Stevedoring Company, did not impress Sarah in the slightest. If Sarah had anything to do with it, this skeleton would be safely locked away, and never allowed to even peek from its wardrobe. Sarah had also warned her father, that, to day of all days, he must not to have any reminiscing about the docks or the men who worked there over the years, especially in his after dinner speech.

They had met in Jurys Hotel on the Western Road four years ago almost to the day. James' company was holding an introduction night for a new brand of Australian wine. Her boyfriend at the time was considered an expert on wines, and was there in a professional capacity. Although Sarah tagged along with Michael to these gatherings, she had no intention of ever ending up with him. There was no doubt that he was what all her friends called a hunk. Good looks, suave manner, impeccably dressed, and a head of hair many men would kill for. If not careful, one might easily fall head over heels in love with him. But! Cautious Sarah had no intention of letting this happen. She felt he had not the bank balance, and he didn't have enough savvy to know how to improve it to Sarahs satisfaction. He was a happy go lucky fellow and took life as it came.

So when Sarah spotted James, she made a few discreet inquiries as to his marital status, his business etc. Michael introduced them, and the kiss on each cheek from James lingered that split second longer than was usual. An introductory kiss, as this was, was normally a quick peck. This was no quick peck, and Sarah decided to cast her net in his direction. She eventually landed her quarry hook, line, and sinker, and after awhile fell hopelessly in love with James.

Everything looked just right. Sarahs dress, bought on a four day trip to Paris earlier in the year, was white ankle length off the shoulder and looked as if she had been poured into the garment. She felt so good in it. The three bridesmaids' dresses, also ankle length and off the shoulder, were bought in one of the top boutiques in Dublin. These three friends of Sarah were her best pals, and had been, right up through Primary, Secondary, and University where Sarah had graduated with a Bachelors Degree in arts. One of James' brothers would be the bestman, two of his brothers and Sarahs brother Daniel were the groomsmen.

When Sarah had finished at college, she went to London where she studied to become a beauty technician. This was a two year course and when she had graduated came back to Cork and started her own business. She aquired a lease, with the option to buy, on a large first floor premises in the upper class suburb of Rochestown Road. A big plus with this location was, that there was parking for twelve cars. Sarah made sure that the guest list on the opening evening was chosen with care. The opening was performed by the then Lord Mayor councillor Jim O'Mahony, and each lady at the opening received a 50.oo voucher. This would ensure that they would return and hopefully become the backbone of the venture. This 50.oo voucher proved to a very profitable investment.

The wedding ceremony would take place in the large gazebo at the bottom of the lawn of their newly acquired home. The house had five bedrooms with each bedroom ensuite. It had a dining room, sitting room, very large built in kitchen, conservatory facing south, and, set in around two acres of landscaped grounds. Already in the gazebo, a string quartet was set up, and playing a varied programme of Jazz, Popular, and Classical music. The reception would be in the Marquee erected at the rear of the house, with a covered passage leading to the kitchen. Caterers and staff were hired for the day and they would look after the food and drink. Already champagne and wine were in the coolers and placed conveniently around the huge table in the Marquee. By some standards it wouldn't be a very big affair, around 100 guests, but, these were mostly the cream of Cork high society. There were of course some of James' family as well, but only those who really had to be invited. A few of his aunts, uncles, his mother and two sisters, and some of his business friends and their wives.

A red carpet was rolled out down the lawn from the sitting room of the house as far as the gazebo. Her father would walk Sarah on this carpet to the gazebo, and hand her over to James. It wouldn't be a full Mass, just some sacred readings appropriate to the occasion and the union blessed by the church. Fr.Molloy a friend of the family would perform the ceremony. A red carpet was also laid down from the gazebo to the marquee. When the meal would be over and the speeches finished, the Marquee would be cleared, and a Glen Millar style eight- piece band would entertain until midnight. Then a Disk Jockey and his disco music would take over until 2.00am or if wanted he would stay later.

Up in her bedroom Sarah with two of her bridesmaids was feeling somewhat excited and nervous. Her two friends assured her she had never looked more beautiful than right now, and truly she had never felt so beautiful than right now. James would be proud of her when he took her hand from her father, and walked her to the altar set up in the gazebo, where Fr. Molloy would be waiting to welcome them. She had a Vodka and tonic to calm her nerves, but she was still very nervous. She wouldn't have any more alcohol, as she didn't want to walk down the isle half sloshed.

Orla the third bridesmaid came into the room where the other two were giving the final touches to Sarahs tiara and train, and said,

"Guess who's just arrived in the kitchen?"

The three stared at her and exclaimed,

"Who?"

"Michael Billington the wine man. It seems he's the caters wine buyer and is checking to make sure every thing is O.K."

"Call my brother Daniel." Said Sarah softly, but sharply.

When Daniel arrived, Sarah explained that Michael her ex boyfriend had arrived in the kitchen. Would Daniel go immediately to the kitchen, and make sure that he was gone from there as quickly as possible. She didn't want anything, or anybody screwing up this day on her. Daniel, who was the soul of diplomacy and discretion in affairs like this, went to the kitchen and soon ushered Michael on his way. Michael wanted to wish Sarah and James the best of luck before leaving, but Daniel explained that at this late stage this was impossible. He would pass on Michaels best wishes to them, and he left rather reluctantly.

James' mother, who didn't quite approve of this sort of thing, and two sisters arrived, and were shown to their appropriate places. Some aunts, uncles, and friends of James also sat in the grooms side. His mother who didn't like Sarah a whole lot, sat there thinking,

'Why couldn't he get married like everyone else in a proper church with a proper Mass. This is just a sham to please that snobbish bitch.' However, if they were happy together, she supposed in the end this was really all that mattered. If his father, who was a very religious man, were still alive he would grow horns, and in all probability would not attend the wedding. To think that a son of his would not marry with the full blessing of the Catholic Church, would in his mind not be married at all.

If Sarah had her way there would be no mixing of the troops, each had their space and hopefully they would stick to their assigned space. At last James arrived with the best man and sat just outside the Gazebo and waited for Sarah to make an appearance. The priest came and had a few words with James, then went into the Gazebo to make sure all the paraphernalia for the ceremony was present and correct.

In the sitting room Sarah and her dad were just about to motion to the quartet to strike up the wedding march, when James rose quickly from his seat. He moved towards where the catering staff had gathered to watch, and stopped opposite one of the uniformed waitresses. Sarah stepped outside the room to see what was happening.

'What the hell is going on?' What is he doing with that creature?'

James had caught the girl by the arm and guided her away from the crowd. Obviously she knew him, as she didn't put up any opposition to being lead to one side. Sarah looked inquiringly at her father. Her father put up his hands in a gesture of ignorance, he hadn't a clue either as to what was going on. Sarah called again for Daniel. When he arrived she explained what had happened and ushered him off to see what the situation was. In the meantime James and the girl had moved to secluded part of the lawn and were chatting when Daniel arrived on the scene. Ever the diplomat Daniel enquired,

"Is there anything wrong? Something awry in the kitchen?"

James answered.

"No this an old friend of mine whom I haven't seen in years. I got the surprise of my life when I saw her. Kathy, this is Daniel, Sarah's brother. Daniel, Catherine Sheehan."

"How do you do Catherine. You know James, everyone's waiting, the only one missing is you. Your bride is waiting to walk down the isle. I'm sure you and Kathy will find plenty of time to chat later on."

James his mind racing hesitated for a second. Then said softly.

"O.K. Kathy we'll talk after the meal."

On his way back to the gazebo, he thought,

'What timing! After how long? Must be at least five years since he and Kathy dated, and now, for her to turn up at this point in time. He had wondered about Kathy a number of times over those five years. Where had she gone to? Never met up with her in the usual social circles. It was as if she had disappeared from the face of the earth, or at least had left for foreign parts. Now here she was again, at what for him, couldn't be a worse time. '

Their breaking up was to say the least, for him, a little traumatic. At that time he was sure Kathy was the woman for him. Then he met Sarah, and he had dated her on a kind of a rebound. He didn't fancy her all that much, but as the years passed, love blossomed between himself and Sarah. And now shortly they would be exchanging vows, and proclaiming their love to all and sundry.

The quartet started playing the wedding march and startled him out of his reverie. The bridesmaids were coming down the red carpet heading for the gazebo, followed by Sarah and her dad and two pageboys that were really trying to keep Sarahs' train off the ground. They failed miserably as the train was too long and too heavy for them.

'My God she looks stunning. What a lucky man I am.'

Her father smiled as he put her hand in James' and turned to join his wife in the front seat.

While all this was happening Daniel had not been idle. He approached the head of the catering staff, pointed at Kathy and asked if she could be sent away. He would personally pay her wages, and if necessary a little extra as well. This person approached Kathy explained the situation and said she would have to leave, but she would be more than compensated for the upset, also this would not interfere with her future employment with his company. Kathy looked at Daniel and if looks could kill, he would be dead inside two seconds flat. She removed her apron threw it on the table and left.

When Daniel eventually got to the gazebo the ceremony was almost over. The bride and groom had exchanged rings. Then the priest gave the union his final blessing and said.

"You may kiss the bride."

Everyone stood and applauded loudly.

As they left the gazebo the quartet played "Here comes the Bride." And they walked up the other red carpet to the marquee. The photographer stopping them about half way to take some pictures of just themselves, and some with family. On reaching the marquee they were directed to the top table, and then members of the two families were seated on both sides of them. Sarah not able to contain herself any longer, asked very softly but bitterly. .

"James what the hell was going on before the ceremony? Just as I was about to walk to the altar with my father, you up and went to talk with some girl on the hired staff."

"She was a friend whom I had not seen for a number of years, and I got a surprise when I spotted her. However I got a bigger surprise when I saw her dressed as a waitress. I was just about to have a few words with her when Daniel intervened. So I said I would meet her after the ceremony and the meal."

This didn't cut any ice with Sarah, and she retorted.

"Seeing you rush off at that precise moment didn't look well to me or to our friends. Did you not hear the murmuring that went up when you left, most thinking you had got cold feet and that I was going to be left at the altar."

"O.K. I was wrong, but Sarah, don't make a song and dance about it. Surely you must have enough faith and trust in me by now to know that I would not do anything to harm our relationship, and that you are the only one for me. I will speak to her after the meal when all the speeches and formalities are over, and I assure you that is all there will be to it."

The quartet moved into the marquee and played softly during the meal. When the speeches, the reading of emails and cards was finished, some more photographs were taken. The tables were cleared all chairs pushed to the side, and the band set up their instruments. It was now eight o'clock in the evening. During the meal James kept looking out for Kathy, but to no avail. While Sarah was otherwise engaged he slipped into the kitchen and enquired about Kathy. He was told she had to leave urgently earlier in the evening, and they hadn't expected her to return.

Disappointed and perplexed by this, James returned to the marquee. He never suspected that Kathy because of his speaking to her before the ceremony, had been, thanks to Daniel, given the bums rush. Not wanting to be caught up in any controversy those of the catering staff that knew of the shafting of Kathy, were warned to keep quiet about the incident.

The band started with the Anniversary Waltz and a big cheer went up as James and Sarah took the floor. They waltzed a few rounds of the floor, and then were joined by other couples. It was truly a most enjoyable night, Around eleven o'clock the wedding cake was cut and a slice was given to each with some tea or coffee. Close to midnight a human arch was made and James and Sarah went through to the chanting of "For they are jolly good fellows." At the end of the arch James mum and Sarahs mum and dad were waiting to give them one last hug, and they ran to where a limousine was waiting to take them their hotel. From the hotel they would go to the airport in the morning, and fly to Silver Sands, Jamaica to spend the next two weeks on honeymoon there.

As he placed his arm around Sarah in the back of the limo, James put all thoughts of Kathy from his mind. The past was now in the past, and whatever the future held, Sarah and he would face it together. He had, he hoped, found true love with Sarah and felt that they would have a wonderful future together. Sarah uttered a sigh of relief as she relaxed into James arms. Looking back over the day Sarah thought for a while. It looked as if this wedding would not take place. She knew she had panicked over some small insignificant incidents that at the time looked rather major, but turned out to be just a storm in a tea cup. She nestled her face into James' neck, and gently kissed him. It was the perfect ending to an almost perfect day.

Quirke of Fate

Do you wake up each morning to the same routine. Get out of bed supposedly feeling refreshed, but really in worse shape than when you went to bed the night before.

You shave, shower etc., and head for the kitchen, picking up the mail on the way. The mail is heavy this morning, thanks to it being about 90% junk. Most of this you consign to the rubbish container without even opening it. Shake out the cereal, put on the kettle, place two slices of bread in the toaster, and have the cereal while this is toasting.

"Guess Helen is having a lie in this morning. It's fine for her, being her own boss."

You switch on the radio and listen to the news. But! Are you really taking in all the news' reader has to say? Are you listening and not hearing? You probably don't have that much interest in any case, but the news' reader drones on.

A plane has crashed somewhere over North America, all 360 passengers and crew are feared dead. A ferry has capsized off one of the islands that make up the Philippines. There are some survivors, but bad weather is hampering rescue efforts. A bus crashes in India, those not killed instantly were burned alive in the inferno that followed. A bomb meant for somewhere in London explodes prematurely, while being transported to its target on a public service bus, killing ten people including the carrier. Then there are wars and the rumours of wars.

You are listening to this, but are you really taking it all in. After all how could it effect you? You'll be heading out shortly and driving the five miles or so to work. Then for eight hours you'll sit and gaze at a computer screen that blurts out information about someone or other. Some of this information is so private that it is a breach of business ethics that it should be kept on disk at all. Well! One never knows when a little subtle pressure may be needed to sway opinions in your favour.

In our every day life many of us irrespective of our profession, find our job boring and unfulfilling. If it weren't for the money it brings in we wouldn't be found dead in such a job. Of course the other fellows job is always the best.

Thinking back to the night before, and the row you had with Helen, wasn't it really money orientated, and should never have happened. Then, isn't money your biggest problem? Will there ever be enough? Both of you are so busy making money that having a family is way in the future. Whatever the reason you shouldn't have left the house this morning without trying to resolve the argument, and start the new day afresh. An old Irish saying goes "Never let the sun set on harsh words, they will look much worse when the it rises."

No, stubbornness prevailed, so here you are driving along and promising you will fix everything when you return home in the evening.

Take her out for a nice meal and a drink. Maybe talk about starting a family.

What was that the news reader said, something about a school somewhere in Scotland where a number of children were murdered by this crazy guy with a high powered rifle. Well, never mind, all these disasters are so far away that they could not possibly have any bearing on your life. Then maybe that's how some of these people were thinking yesterday.

A high rise crane is lifting a pallet of bricks to the top of a building. Despite all the precautions that were taken before the actual lifting, one brick falls from the pallet. As it falls to the ground gathering speed at every foot a pedestrian just ambling along on the footpath is hit on the head and killed.

An Artic truck leaves Belfast docks at 6.30am to travel to Dublin with its load of steel. An American and his wife left their home in New York the evening before to fly to Ireland. They leave Dublin airport at 8.30am the following morning in their hired car and head for Dublin City. At a particularly hazardous junction both vehicles collide with tragic results for the American and his wife.

So, what placed these two bodies, the truck and its driver, the car and its two occupants, in this position that they should meet so tragically at this precise second in time? Two separate entities from two different cultures, suddenly, becoming part of the one statistic.

Should we not sit up and take more notice of these incidents, and think, 'What could it have possibly been that had brought them together?

Was it Fate? Was it coincidence? An act of God? A freak accident? Just plain bad luck? Or a combination of all?

We often sound so pompous and say we control our own destiny. But, how much control do we really have? If we stop to think about how much control we possess, it may be rather frightening to realise we possess very little, or indeed none at all. We are indeed far from being masters of our own destiny. You leave your workplace in the evening and drive down the highway towards home. Your head is throbbing. It's full of numbers and figures confusing your mind, and this goddamn traffic is getting to you as well. How can there be so many idiots on one stretch of roadway?

However there is one consolation, you've phoned Helen and you'll go for a drink and a meal after you arrive home. You're happy about this.

Then the mobile phone rings.

"Hello, Yes this is Declan."

"But I'm half home now. O.K O.K. I'll turn at the next roundabout and go back.

You put the phone away and murmur to yourself,

"Shag Mike and his disk. The one day I wanted to be home on time. Well never mind it won't take too long. Half an hour won't make much difference. Something very important must have cropped up when he can't wait until morning. Shag him anyway.

Coming up to the roundabout, you go right around and travel back on the other carriageway. You give the pedal an extra push to speed things up a bit. This has put a bit of pressure on you that you could well have done without. What did that sign you just passed say?

"Slow danger ahead." Or was it a roadside add?

"Oh my God, It's an oil spillage. That truck where did it come from?"

You stamp on the brakes, and as the back of the truck looms up before you, you see the look of disbelief on the faces of the council workers as they scatter in all directions. Helens face appears before you and you scream, "Oh no!"

And then you become part of the 10.00 o'clock news.

Stressing the Point

How many of us can say with any degree of certainty, that is of course if we're still alive,

"That's grand I'll see you here in two weeks time" or is it "If I'm not working late I'll see you" or "If I have the time I'll meet you."

We have become so dependant on the need to work, that any little time we can salvage outside work time, just to sit and talk, or attend fortnightly Toastmasters meetings, is a bonus instead of a priority.

Yet every day we hear of some friend or other who has collapsed because of stress or some stress related ailment. We may well remark " How foolish they've been" and that they were really only "living to work."

That he or she never left their place of work without bringing some project with them to be completed at home. This is usually very much to the detriment of family life. When we close the office door, or the garage gates, or pull down the warehouse shutters how many of us can leave the work behind?

How many of us on shutting up shop on Friday evening or whenever, make sure that first the mobile phone is turned on? This is just in case some one will want to ring in a last minute order, or to check that a certain fax has been received, or for confirmation that their specific needs are being given priority.

How many people will you see driving along with one hand on the steering wheel and the other holding a mobile phone to their ear, more than likely these are still doing business in this highly dangerous and illegal fashion. I imagine it has been the cause of many a bumper to bumper collision?

I was having breakfast recently in a hotel when this young lady came and sat at the next table. Dressed in a beautifully tailored costume, complete with blouse and shoes to match and with her brief case, which she placed on the chair beside her, she looked every inch the executive type. As they would say back in West Cork,

"God! But isn't she the real lad."

The waiter came she ordered breakfast, and sat sipping her orange juice. Around one minute elapsed when I heard the "Bleep, bleep" of a mobile phone. It was hers. After a short conversation she immediately cancelled breakfast,

"As" she said "something has cropped up." Her demeanour quickly changed, and the stress of the situation was clearly visible on her face as she hurriedly left. This was just 7.20 in the morning.

'My God' I thought 'What a way to start the day.'

Another day I was in the toilet of a well known city hotel and I heard the familiar "Bleep, Bleep" coming from one of the cubicles, and this guy caught in

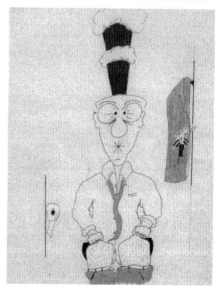

mid air answering the call of nature, also had to answer the phone. I would think that for him, constipation looked a good option.

At mass one Sunday while the priest was giving the sermon, off goes a mobile. This was to the obvious amusement of the congregation, but to chagrin of one gentleman, an undertaker by trade. He quickly left the church followed by the glares of the preacher. In our

parish he is now known as the "Dead Ringer." I'm sure if I were to carry one of those things myself, I would probably get stressed out just waiting for it to ring.

The home telephone is another instrument that can add enormously to stress, especially if you're the one who rarely gets a call. It seems to ring incessantly, and always it seems with such urgency that one can never ignore it. How often have I sat down with my wife to have a cup of tea and a chat, but as soon as the kettle whistles, the phone rings and must be answered. I have come to the conclusion that in some mysterious way our telephone is connected to the kettle.

The television, a wonderful invention in its own right, but has it become a necessity in a lot of homes. How many homes have only one television? I think the answer to this would surprise us. Many of the people I know have a portable in the kitchen, and a number of them have got one in the bedroom as well. The number of channels we can now receive is mind bending, yet, we can still only watch one at the time, but at least, unlike the telephone we can turn the tele off.

As someone who has, Thank God, worked all his life, I now realise that the first hours overtime was the worst hour I ever worked. From then on I couldn't live without overtime, and before I knew where I was Saturday or Sunday, or even both, were a must. The washing machine, fridge, dryer, microwave, car, all had to be paid for and when paid for, still needed extra money to keep them running. It was a vicious circle and one never seemed to be able to make the two ends meet, or indeed, make them come close to meeting.

Everyday in the newspapers, and at night on the tele, we're being drip fed and sometimes bombarded with information about a whole lot of modern contraptions, and people trying to persuade us that we cannot possibly live without them. Each is a must for the modern home. All these pressures tend to upset us and may cause us a great deal of stress. It tends to make us feel that we're not living at all, when what we really need is what the Americans call "A little quality time." Time to shut everything off and have a good old fashioned family chat, or maybe not to talk at all. Just to sit and feel the closeness of your loved ones around you, and feel snugly wrapped in a radiance of love.

So I would say to you "Think about this, and consider turning off the mobile, disconnect the phone, pull the plug on the tele, put the kettle on and enjoy a nice cuppa, with some home made scones with a good dollop of butter, and a lash of blackberry jam. I think that you may find that although the best things in life may not be free, they beat being stressed out hands down.

Careering Along

Are the best hurlers sitting on the ditch? Are back seat drivers the real experts? Where ignorance is bliss is it really folly to be wise. This I won-der about at times. Even though I've been a professional driver for nearly half a century, I find that young people to-day, who are still in the L plate class, tend to lecture me on the rights and wrongs of driving. With their provisional license in their pocket they know it all.

I don't think that driving comes naturally to anyone. It is a skill that needs a fair amount of tuition. Our roads are getting better but our cars are getting faster, and despite all the built-in safety measures more accidents occur, and more people are being maimed and injured on our roads. Why are some reluctant to switch on their lights as fog moves in or evening approaches? When I asked a young driver about this, he told me,

"I have no problem seeing where I'm going, so why should I be wasting my battery?"

But! Surely it is as important to be seen as to be able to see? We don't all have 20 – 20 vision. I have in my time driven most types of vehicles, from combine harvesters to excavators, cranes, forklifts, coaches, and even the odd old bicycle. Still when I come up against these new high-tech high-spec jockeys, I find I am lost in the new jargon and car speak of our modern youth. I remember when something went wrong with the car a few years ago, one would open up the bonnet, look at the engine, spot the trouble, fiddle around a bit, and off it would go again.

This has changed somewhat however, and now if anything goes wrong with the modern car you've got to get it to the garage, connect it to a computer and wait for a read out, and then from that, try and figure out what's the matter with it. Some cars are so complicated that if anything does happen you may as well change it. Because by the time the garage is finished, it would probably be cheaper to trade it in for a new model.

I don't know why I've got so hung up on all this car technology, when all I wanted to do was to tell you a couple of incidents that happened to me as a driver.

The first time I went to the United States I was genuinely in awe of this great country. The amount of heavy goods vehicles on the roads there is, for one from Ireland -- a mind-boggling experience. There didn't seem to be any end to them. Like "Old Man River, they just keep rolling along." On our second week there my friend asked if we would like to see a Baseball game. We had had never seen the game of baseball before except in some film so we said " Sure, why not."

"O.K." he says. "Tomorrow evening the Orioles are playing the New York Yankees in Baltimore we'll take a run up there."

Next evening we left Silver Spring and travelled to Baltimore. It was I remember a very pleasant journey on a lovely summers evening. Arriving at the stadium car park, my friend Derek opened the trunk of the car and took out a cooler full of Budweiser beer and a few soft drinks. He also had a bucket of Kentucky fried chicken, and on our way in he purchased a bucket of Popcorn. One could be forgiven at this stage for thinking that it was a picnic we were going to instead of a Baseball game.

The size of the stadium took my breath away, just endless rows of seats circling a huge oval ring. One could hardly see what they call the diamond it was so far down in a hollow. A p.a. system was blaring out information about players, their past performances, and as each player was mentioned a great roar went from the crowd. The atmosphere was fantastic, with the rival fans shouting abuses at each other. As each player came to take his position at batting or pitching, the roar or the booing from the crowd was deafening.

What impressed me a lot about the evening was, that it seemed to be an evening out for all the family, and each family had their popcorn, beer, soft drinks, and fried chicken. All were decked out in the colours of their favourite team. The game, which I thought was rather boring, and lasted around three hours, eventually finished. As they say in the States,

" The game ain't over 'till the fat Lady sings."

I thought on this night that she was never going to sing. We made our way to the car park and put our almost empty containers in the trunk. During the game we had scoffed most of the chicken, all of the popcorn, and they, my friend and his wife, had finished the Budweiser between them. Mary and myself are total abstainers, we had just a few soft drinks.

My friend Derek turns to me and says, in fairly slurred speech, "Paddy you've got to drive home. Mags and I have had too much to drink."

"What!" I exclaimed. "I can't drive home, I've never driven a Chevvy automatic, I've never driven on the right hand side of the road, I've never driven a vehicle with the steering wheel on the left hand side, and worst of all I haven't a clue how to get back to Silver Spring."

"It's no problem" he says "It's only about 50 miles, I'll keep my eye on you and make sure you don't make any wrong turns. All you have to do is drive out of the car park, take a right at the next junction, and head for Interstate 95. After that it's all down hill."

Interstate 95 I remembered on the way down was a five lane high-way, inhabited by lunatics that would make Eddie Irvine look like a Sunday driver. I looked at Mary we both shrugged out shoulders, and sat into the car.

"Oh yes," He slurred when we had the motor running. "Another thing, that little black ball on the dashboard with the white letters and numbers keep your eye on that. Make sure the needle is pointing South at all times, and you can't go wrong." This was a small compass, you know one of those things that are usually about 95% wrong.

So here we go. We get out of the car park and hopefully head for Interstate 95, Derek in his slurred alcoholic voice giving directions. We were on or way and again hopefully, going in the right direction. We moved along nicely and very carefully, with me wishing it were St, Christopher and not that damn compass was on the dashboard. What made it really hard was, that you have to keep remembering that the car is all on your right hand side and not on the left, the side you are familiar with. I cling to the steering wheel and try to keep in the lane as best I can. Then a very large sign appears which says, "Tunnel ahead, please keep at 50 mph."

"My God" I shouted "Derek it's the tunnel, I'll never make it through"

No response from the back seat. I look at the speedometer and bring it up to 50 it feels like I'm doing 150. In we go into the tunnel, not looking left or right, just straight ahead. Hands grasping the steering wheel, knuckles white as chalk, perspiration flowing freely down my body, so much so, that soon I am sitting in a pool of sweat. All this was adding to my discomfort. It wasn't a nice short tunnel like Jack Lynchs tunnel in Cork. Oh no! It was very long and very badly lit.

'My God.' I thought to myself, 'I'm in the only tunnel in the world with no light at the end.'

After what seemed like an eternity we eventually exited and came out on to a highway with so many directional signs that it was almost impossible to pick out 95. I gazed at the compass, and this was impossible to decipher as it juggling around like jelly. Alternating between the four points.

I called to the back seat "Derek which way?"

His response a loud gutteral, "Snore, snore."

I shouted at my sister "Mags, help." Again all I got from her was "Snore, snore."

Then Mary exclaimed. "Pat that sign it says Interstate 95 South." We turned left at the next intersection, and felt we were at least going in the right direction.

On we drove. I'm in a bog of sweat and visibly shaking. Nerves on edge, and not one bit happy. After a few more near misses and someone shouting across the carriage - way from a pick-up truck,

"Get off the road and go back home you bloody Leprechaun."

Then trying to get through major junctions with traffic lights swinging precariously up in the·air, we make our way to Silver Spring and into Snowdrop Lane. I drive the car into the car port, put on the hand brake, cut the motor and breathe a big sigh of relief. Mary smiles and says this is something to tell the grandchildren when we get back. Then a voice from the back seat croaks,

"Wake up Mags we're home. That was great, never minded the journey at all. Paddy I knew you could do it."

I said nothing. Even though it was past midnight, I went straight away to have a shower and change. I was thankful for making the journey home safely, but also I was bent on giving both of them a bit of my mind. When I went in to the sitting room to do this, the television was on and there the both of them were, quite comfortable sitting in their armchairs, snoring their brains out. And here I am, too stressed out to even get my eyes to close.

Old Age Ha! Ha! Ha!

I ask the question is anyone old anymore? Has Senior Citizenship become more than a state of mind? Rather than waiting for the undertaker to arrive has it become a new dawning? Look around you, people in retirement have become so active that for some there are not enough hours in the day.

Time was when retirement cast a shadow as we felt that finishing work meant finishing with life. But now there are so many associations with so many activities available that retirement could be just the name for the dog. In most parishes there is a Senior Citizen Club and these provide a lot of activities such as Indoor Bowling, Painting Classes, Bingo, Cards, Dancing, good old fashioned Sing – Songs and other activities.

There are, some people as you know, who have found it very hard to make friends as they went through life. Yet, they have found when coming into contact with a Senior Citizen club, what ever inhibitions they've previously had disappeared fairly quickly. They become part and parcel of their new environment, and avenues they never thought existed open up to them.

At last society has become aware of, and has learned to accommodate the Senior Citizen. If Social Welfare is not enough for one to survive on, you have the supplementary welfare allowance, and so poverty for the aged may be avoided. There are other schemes as well to help, and all these go to make life a little easier for those of us who have passed our sell by date. They are also taking part in many community projects, in these they have shown that their life experiences can be of great benefit to those starting out on lifes journey.

In my job as a Coach Driver [You know sometimes when I say this, someone is nearly always bound to say "Do you drive two horses or four] I drive Senior Citizens to different places and functions. How they look forward to these outings. When they go out they go out to have a ball and no holds barred. They show as much enthusiasm for these trips as any school kid does. I'll give you two anecdotes from one particular trip.

7.45am at Douglas Court to pick up 40 Senior Citizens and transport them to the Phoenix Park. Even though there's still 15 minutes to boarding time, there are at least 25 waiting to board. In this group there are two sisters who go through the same routine each time before the coach leaves. One stands on the footpath and makes signs to the one inside. Now the first time I saw this happen I couldn't figure out what they were at. So I asked the one inside if she were alright, and she says to me.

"We don't want to be sitting on the wheel."

"You need have no fear" I said "We in Cronins' Coaches don't allow anyone to sit on the wheel, all our passengers are accommodated on nice comfortable seats inside the coach."

"Oh!" she explained "I meant we didn't want to be sitting over the wheel."

Some more arrived and got on board and this lady says to me "Where is the best place to sit sir I'm a very bad traveller."

"Look" I said "We have a 350 mile round trip and you're a very bad traveller. Here's a plastic bag and when you feel you're getting sick, stick your head into this and do not mess up the carpet."

We arrived at Árus an Úachtarán around 1.00 o'clock and went in to meet the president. I found President McAlise truly a beautiful person, the way she met and shook hands and had a word with each one. Then she accompanied them to where they were served tea and nice cookies. Everyone seemed to be really taken by her. After this we were given a guided tour of the house. When this was finished the president accompanied them to the front door and wished them a safe journey home.

On getting on the coach again everyone except one woman was on a high after the experience. I asked her did she not enjoy it, and she answered,

"I'm disappointed after coming all this way that we didn't meet the president himself. But still isn't Hillary lovely."

We left Dublin and headed for home stopping on the way to have a meal. After the meal they had a few drinks and were in good form for the rest of the journey. We had a great sing – song and some came up to the microphone and done their party piece. Some of these people were in their late seventies and early eighties but acted as if they were only in their late twenties. For me it was an eye opener, and the words of that well known Liam Clancy ballad rang in my ears.

"It's never too late to start living, to get up and have some fun, for the sun will be just as shiny in the morning, as the first day the world began."

And again the moral of the story is, "It's never too late to start living."

The Odd Couple

"Good morning Tim, come in I'll be with you in a minute, It looks like a fine morning outside."

" Hiya Jackie, 'tis indeed a lovely morning, a bit chilly though. I hope it stays that way for the match."

"Good morning Tim sit down, will you have a cuppa, there's fresh tea in the pot?"

"No Lou thanks, it would only spoil me for the couple of pints after mass."

"The two of you are well met, ye're whole world revolves around a couple of pints."

"Any luck in the Lotto last night Lou? A handy win, over two and a half million. I had the first three out and no more. It's the story of my life Lou, always short one for a few bob."

"I had no luck either Tim, I done a quick pick, one number is all I had. Wisha Tim God send us no greater loss boy, we might be better off with out all that money."

" I don't know all the same Lou, I'd love to have one whip off it. Money is something if you think you have too much of it you can get rid of it easily enough. What a feeling it must be to be a millionaire, without ever again to be scrapin' and scroungin' or wonderin' where next weeks rent is coming from."

"Yerra Tim it has been the cause of the breaking up of many families too. Wouldn't the Deasys up the road be better off if their father hadn't won it three years ago, sure it broke that family up completely, and sent their mother to an early grave."

"Even after that Lou I think I'd still take a chance."

"Right Tim let's go"

"O.K. Jackie, see you later Lou."

"'Bye Tim, say one for me."

"Of course I will Lou, and one for Jackie too."

The two friends head down the street towards their parish church.

"Well Jackie I hope it's the new priest Fr. Hannigan says mass this morning. That Fr. O'Reilly would try the patience of Job.

"Tim we're not in the church yard yet and you're starting to criticise. It doesn't matter who the priest is, we have the day long, and the mass will only take at most 45minutes. So Tim no more yapping please."

"O.K. Jackie boy end of story."

It's Sunday morning, two old pals Jackie and Tim take up their usual position for Sunday Mass at the end of stairs that leads up to the gallery. Although great friends, they are complete opposites. They are the epitome of the "Odd Couple." Jackie, a tall slim quiet easy going fellow who when he meets a woman acquaintance on the street respectfully doffs his hat. His best friend Tim, low sized, stout, and a bit of a rough diamond wouldn't bid them the time of day. He usually finds fault with everyone and everything around him.

The priest Fr. O'Reilly comes on the altar with his two altar servers, places the chalice in position, kisses the altar, genuflects, and looks sternly down the church.

"Good morning everyone."

"Good morning father."

"In the name of the Father and of the Son and of the Holy Spirit."

"Amen."

"You're all very welcome here this fine morning to join in our celebration of the Holy Eucharist."

"The Lord be with you."

"And also with you."

"Today my good people is the 3rd Sunday of Advent, and all our thoughts must be on the coming of the saviour. It is of course for us a very special time of the year when we must shake off the old mantle, and don the mantle of reconciliation and grace --------"

"There he is Jackie off on one of his tantrums, that Fr. O'Reilly thinks we have nothing else to do but to stand here while he gives a sermon before, during, and after mass. He's murder Jackie boy, some day I'm going to tape him and post him the tape, it might lighten him up a bit, although I don't think that's possible. It's no wonder that a lot of the youngsters are skipping mass these days, can you blame them with the likes of that man on the altar."

"Now, now Tim, Fr. O'Reilly is a very spiritual and learned man, and whatever he talks about he always speaks with great knowledge and authority. He's a plain speaker Tim. You could say a speaker for the people, and he's always loud and clear. I like him."

"You want to know something Jackie boy I think he just loves the sound of his own voice. I think he believes his voice is music to our ears. Well Jackie I've heard a lot sweeter tunes."

"Easy now Tim, I'm beginning to think you and he have a lot in common. You're not exactly tongue tied yourself you know, sometimes you remind me of one who has been injected with a gramophone needle. And Tim please remember where you are"

"I know where I am alright Jackie boy, but Fr. O'Reilly thinks he's up on a podium talking down to us peasants. High falutin' that's what he is. 'Twould be more in his line if he put in a bit of heating here at the back door, I don't think he thinks much of us punters hangin' in back here. A fella could freeze to death down at this end of the church, after all whether he likes it or not we're part of his congregation too. I bet it's fine and warm up where he is. Betcha there's no fear of him ceasing up from hypothermia."

"Stop it Tim I'll not have you talking about Fr. O'Reilly like that especially during mass. If anyone hears you, you might be brought up for slander. Now how would you like that? Have a small bit of cop on."

"O.K. Jackie boy I'll shut up."

"Please be seated for to-days readings. The first reading is a reading from the book of Isaiah and tells us of the joyful expectations for the future."

"The second reading is taken from the book of Jonah and tells us to be happy at all times as the coming of the Messiah is at hand."

"I ask ye Jackie boy look who's going up to do the readings, Mickey and Doris Maloney, livin' together for 14 years, got married only 2 years ago, have four children from 12 to 4 years old and now their pillars of the church. There's a quare turn about for you."

"Never mind about that Tim just listen to what they have to say. And remember what they say is not their word but the word of God. And I'm sure Tim if you think you can do better, you can volunteer to do that job any Sunday."

"I'd look lovely standin' up there alongside Fr.O'Reilly and him scowlin' at me as if I was trying to do him out of a job. Come 'ere

Jackie who's yer wan in the mini skirt up in the gallery. Is she the wan that serves in whacker Buckleys pub? She looks more like a lap dancer than a barmaid but who's complainin' eh Jackie boy."

"Tim this is not the place for that kind of talk, we're here to attend mass not observe the talent. You're paying more attention to everyone and everything around you, you're not one bit attentive to the mass and that's primarily why we're here. And indeed I'm having a tough time myself trying to concentrate.

"Do you think City will win to day Jackie?" ·

"I don't know Tim, I'm hoping they will, but at the same time I don't know. Tim for Gods sake we're at mass. We'll talk about the game in the pub later."

"You know Jackie I think they'll have the edge alright, still I think it's a bit too close to call. I don't think Bricky Barretts young fellow is on the panel at all to day, he'll be a big loss. He has great speed on the wing."

"Whisht Tim.

"The Lord be with you."

"And also with you."

"To-days Word is taken from the Holy Gospel according to St. Luke."

"When John the Baptist came forth from the wilderness to baptise the multitudes and proclaim the good news --------------''

"This is the gospel of the Lord."

"Praise to you Lord Jesus Christ.".

"Now my dear brethern can anything be more straight forward than today's gospel by St. Luke, it tells us exactly where we should be coming from and where we should be going, it shows exactly where our priorities should lie ------------------''

"O.K. Jackie boy here it is sermon no.2 wake me in 20 minutes when he might be just thinking of finishing. 'Twould be no harm if he was going to the game it might speed him up a bit."

"Tim why do you bother to come to mass at all? You never stop talking and you're always critical of Fr. O'Reilly. He can't help if he's a bit longwinded, he's a very dedicated man. Now shut up Tim I want to hear what he has to say."

"Right Jackie boy give me a shout when he's finished."

"------------ So my friends heed the gospel and the words of St. Luke and go your way in peace."

"Come on Tim I know you're only pretending to be asleep"

"That's just it Jackie, his voice would penetrate through a six inch block wall. We want to have a couple of pints before the dinner, but with him we'll be lucky to make the 'Cross for the game. Well, well Jackie, look who's making the collection this morning, Stinker Johnson. You may be sure he'll have a few pints after mass, compliments of the parish. If I had a corky or a washer I'd put it on the plate. Sure he'd rob the poor box, he would."

"My God Tim is there any shutting you up, you haven't a good word to say for anyone. You're biggest cynic I know."

"I'm only telling the truth Jackie boy and well you know it."

"That's enough for now Tim show a bit of respect, we're just coming up to the consecration."

"This Is My Body.

"This is My Blood."

" Peace be with you."

"And also with you."

"Please stand and pray in the words that Jesus thought us. Our Father who art in Heaven ------------------------"

"For thine is the kingdom the power and the glory"

"Let us now turn and offer each other the sign of peace."

"Many happy returns Jackie boy."

"Look Jackie, look, there's that oul' steamer Casey and his oul' doll going up to give out communion. The two biggest thieves in the Parish, everyone that goes into that shop of theirs is robbed, they stick a penny and tuppence on to everything. I wouldn't mind but it's the ordinary people they rob. Eucharistic ministers me ass."

"Stop it now Tim that's not very nice talk, especially at mass. You are in the house of God you know."

"Jackie boy if their fit to be Eucharistic ministers, I should be a candidate for the Vatican. Those people gall me, Their halos are blindin'."

"Oh Tim please, that's not nice talk and people might hear you. You'll cause a scandal in the parish, and anyway you don't really know anything about Mr. and Mrs. Casey"

"Jackie not alone do I know it, but you know it as well yourself."

"Now listen to what I have to say to you Tim. I should have said this to you a long time ago, but I didn't want to hurt your feelings. This may not be the place to say it but I'm going to say it anyhow. Don't call me for mass anymore. It's just impossible to concentrate with your continuous chatter, and furthermore from next Sunday onwards I'm moving up the church. You can have the stairs and observations all to yourself. I'll meet you in Markys as usual after mass, but I am not attending mass with you anymore. You're becoming one big pain in the butt."

"My God Jackie would you really do that to me after all these years together, I'm surprised and shocked. You're lucky I'm not very sensitive and don't take you seriously. Jackie sure no man, no not even God, could come between us. We're like chalk and cheese Jackie boy, and that's what makes us tick. Here Jackie, what about Lulu? If that happened she'd divorce you and throw you out of the house."

"Please Tim don't call her Lulu call her by her proper name, you know her name is Louise, and again Tim shut up."

"And what about the kids Jackie boy, how their eyes light up when I call, and me the godfather of the eldest fella. Do I ever let them down for a few bob, you'd be in right trouble."

"Now dearly beloved we'll have the second collection in aid of the propagation of the faith."

"Hey Jackie look at the smile on stinkers face, he's on double time today."

"Well my dear brethern we've come to the end of our celebration and just to remind you ---------------"

"Here it is Jackie what did I tell you, this is his third sermon. He should join Toastmasters and learn about timing and brevity, would he ever give us his blessing and let us go."

"---------------------- And dearly beloved let us make this week our special soul saving week."

"The Lord be with you."

"And also with you"

"May the Almighty God bless you, the Father, the Son and the Holy Spirit. Our mass is ended let us go in peace to love and serve the Lord.

And two voices in unison exclaim "Thanks be to God."

Met by Chance?

Paddy O'Sullivan was enjoying a stroll up along the Lee fields, his little jack Russell terrier Prince, chasing the crows and seagulls, with of course never a hope of catching any of them. The sun was shining gloriously and he felt at peace with himself and the world around him. There was he thought a lot to be said for shift work. He couldn't enjoy this morning if he had been working all days. Then he sat on the seat facing the river, admiring the beautiful trees, houses, and lawns on the hillside that sloped gently up from the bank of the river. After a little while he felt a little drowsy and thought to himself.

'My God if only if only I could stop time now.'

A stranger whom he had not seen approaching came and sat down beside him. The stranger was tall, well built, with a beard and fairly long hair. He didn't speak with a Cork accent, and Paddy though fairly good at recognising where people came from could not fathom the strangers' accent at all.

"Good morning, beautiful morning" said the stranger.

"It is indeed Thank God," replied Paddy. A great morning to be alive and have the health and time to enjoy it. You're well yourself?"

"I'm very well thank you, but then, who wouldn't be on a fine morning like this. The Lee valley is truly beautiful"

"True for you indeed. Mind you, you don't look all that happy. You're a bit forlorn looking to me, like someone who is troubled."

"I'm a bit down alright, but as you say it's good to be alive on such a fine morning"

"What is it that upsets you? Is there anything I can do to help?

"I don't know, I feel sad when I see how this old planet Earth is progressing. If one could call it progress. I fear very much for its future. The greed of some is horrendous, it reminds me of Nero fiddling while Rome burns. I'm alright Jack and damn the rest."

" Ah now, hang on a minute, I don't think that it's all that bad, that someone like yourself should be going around looking as if you have the weight of the whole world on your shoulders. Some of it may be depressing, but some very positive things are happening as well."

"Such as?"

"In a number of countries there's the coming together of old enemies, talks are taking place to try and iron out and cure old festering wounds. In our own country there are those who are trying to take the magnitude out of obstacles which up to now seemed insurmountable."

The stranger rubbed his beard thoughtfully and said.

"Aha, in the meantime what about all those starving to death, while others stockpile necessities which would make the difference between life and death for the starving? Man can be very cruel to his own. Some suffer while others live in the lap of luxury. Then, what about the stockpiling of weapons of mass destruction, weapons that would make the Atom Bomb seem like a damp squib? The brain seems to have become a device by which man can, and does, create worldwide misery. His selfishness is destroying the protective ozone layer, his pollution is killing life on rivers, lakes, and seas. It is affecting the very air he breathes, and he gives little or no thought to eternity. He is so arrogant it makes one feel that he believes he's going to live forever. Yet! If you put him in context with the whole cosmic sphere, he's even smaller than a full stop."

"I agree fully with you but I would say to you, would it not be better to provide these starving people with the means by which they could fend for themselves. You know most people don't want handouts."

"That's very noble of you. What do you suggest?"

"I'm afraid my suggestions wouldn't count for much. People in high places may seem to listen attentively to what I have to say, but in reality they do not want to know me or my ideas."

"Then you and others like you must out of necessity stand up and be counted." The stranger countered. "You should come together and use whatever machinery is at your disposal to have your voices heard."

"That's easier said than done. Most of our time is taken up trying to make ends meet, and no matter how hard we try, sometimes we fail miserably. Charity must surely begin at home, and, one cannot lift others boats at the risk of his own foundering. Do you not think this is so?"

"Although charity should begin at home it should never end there. If it does, you are insulating yourself at the risk of the exposure of others. Do you think this is fair?"

"Excuse me, who are you? From the passing of the time of day, this conversation has become a lecture by you on world issues. You're beginning to make me feel I'm responsible for all the illnesses of this world. You look at it from a wider perspective, and you will realise that me and whatever powers I possess, are very insignificant. I'll ask you again who are you?"

"My name is Jesus, what's yours?"

" O'Sullivan, Paddy O'Sullivan, and you are Jesus who?"

"I am Jesus son of Mary and the carpenter Joseph."

"Ha! Ha! Ha! Very good I see it all now. You just happen to be passing this way you meet up with me and say to yourself.2

'Now here's a likely client, I'll have a bit of sport with him.'

"Well Jesus whoever you are you're on the wrong track, because I have neither the time nor the inclination to listen to any more of your ráméish. Oh! And by the way ráméish is Gaelic for nonsense."

"Just like Thomas, doubting my very existence."

"I'm not doubting your existence. After all I can see you, I'm speaking with you, and I don't believe I'm dreaming. It's your credentials I have doubts about."

"Do you always doubt the word of people you meet?"

"Now lets be fair and face facts. I'm sitting here on this riverside bench minding my own business enjoying this beautiful spring morning, you come along sit beside me, and introduce yourself as Jesus of Nazareth . I mean Jesus of Nazareth, come off it now, how naive do you think I am. Then you have the audacity to drag me over the coals because you're not happy with the state of the world. If you are Jesus of Nazareth then you have it in your power, or so we're led to believe, to change the whole Universe, not to mind this little spec of cosmic dust. The least you could do is to provide its inhabitants with enough horse sense to see right from wrong, and allow us to live in some kind of harmony. No matter what you say, or how it looks, we are not better off left to our devises."

"You know I cannot interfere. Man has been given the gift of free will, and interference with that free will, either for good or bad, reduces him to the status of animal who must be either led or driven."

"And don't you think that's what we need now? Most of us can't see beyond our nose, we need a push from some direction. Remember the Apostles followed a miracle man. One who cured the sick, the blind, and the lame, He even brought Lazarus back from the dead. Paul didn't believe anything until he was struck down on the road to Damascus. Peter the most cherished of all, denied ever knowing you until he heard the cock crowing. Even Judas was used to fulfil a prophecy because of his very human failing, greed. In its own way his death, so filled with guilt, was every bit as traumatic as your crucifixion. It was just part of the overall picture. Like painting by numbers, one square at the time until the picture is complete. If all those things didn't happen you would not have died such an awful death. So you see in my opinion there was interference all the way."

Jesus shook his head and was about to say something, but Paddy was now on a roll and kept going.

"Was not Marys Immaculate Conception another contrived incident as was the night you were born. If Joseph had not been so lax he would have arrived in plenty of time for the birth. Instead it is the poor Innkeeper that has gone down in history as the one who forced the Messiah to be born in a stable. Surely it was Joseph and not the Innkeeper who was at fault here. I know there was no telecommunications in those far off days, but couldn't the Lord have sent an angel ahead to alert the Innkeeper. This has happened on a number of occasions and one that comes readily to mind is the apparitions at Fatima in Portugal. An angel was sent ahead to prepare the children for the coming of the Virgin."

There was no stopping Paddy now.

"What about the three wise men? Would they have found their way to Bethlehem if someone had not contrived to have that star shine so brightly that they were able to follow it night and day. Adam and Eve is another case in point. They were placed in the Garden of Eden with everything at their fingertips, to live a life of ease not wanting for anything. Yet! The Lord deprived them, no, forbade them, the one act that would physically consummate their love for each other. Now I ask you was that fair? When they failed to overcome their natural desire, it took the supreme sacrifice of your life to redeem mankind. Again I might add if from the start, they were allowed to explore their human desires and expand their knowledge of each other on their own, you would never have had to die on that cross."

"Wow! Paddy that was some speech. But don't you see if Adam and Eve had kept their covenant with the Lord it would have made them much stronger in body and soul, and they would have been spiritually uplifted by the experience. After a short period, if you like of initiation, to prove them worthy of all that had been given them, the Lord would then have blessed their coupling. The Lord just asked of them to put a little effort into resisting this act and they failed. Their weakness was their downfall."

Paddy was not to be side tracked, he was in full flight again and continued.

"Then there was the parting of the Red Sea, the leading of the Israelites to the Promised Land, saving David from the lions den, turning the Water into Wine, and many other incidents of you stepping in and saving the day. I can't see that if you are Jesus Christ why you can't come again and straighten us out."

"Paddy you have just proved my point about interfering. You have been given all these happenings which you have quoted and called interference, yet you have grave doubts about me, and my kingdom. Don't you think that if you really believed, and by you I mean all of mankind. If you just listened more carefully to the Word that you would see that living on earth is not the be all and end all of everything. If you firmly believed you would know that life here is only a means to an end. Like I said no one is going to live forever."

"O.K. you've got a point we don't listen therefore we do not see, but you must remember we are living in the present. We are continually living with daily disasters such as Hurricanes, Tornadoes, erupting Volcanoes, Famine, Poverty, Wars, and many other horrors. Our lives are so full of all these phenomena that trying to survive them is nearly a full time occupation."

"Now Paddy you've got a very good point too, but who do you call on when faced with any of these phenomena? You call on my Father, on Me, my Mother, or the Saints. When do you talk to your Guardian Angel? You talk to him or her and ask for help only when trouble looms. Which means he or she is used as a crutch to lean on in times of trouble. Do you ever think of talking to your Guardian Angel when times are good, and thank him or her for their help in times of crisis."

"No! In the good times Paddy your guardian angel, or, whoever you pray to in critical times is non existent. The world would be a much better place if humans were aware at all times of their spiritual friends. Believe me your Guardian Angel is always at your shoulder, and has been instrumental in saving you from mishap a lot more times than you give him or her credit for. Even though you are not aware of his presence he or she is always there. Ready, willing, and able."

"Remember it is not my Father or I who is the cause of these famines and wars, it is mans greed. So open your eyes and look at the overall picture and this will become very clear to you. You must get your priorities right when it comes to differentiating

"Well Paddy I must go now, I have enjoyed our little chat and I have the feeling we'll meet again. In the meantime keep in mind what we were talking about, and don't be afraid to stand up and be counted. Be sure not to forget that your Guardian Angel is always at your shoulder, talk to him."

The stranger walked away and seemed to fade into the surroundings. Prince yapping and pulling at his trouser leg suddenly brought him back to his riverside seat. Paddy stood up from the seat and walked in the other direction and wondered if his mind had lapsed for awhile. Had his imagination run riot, had he been just day dreaming, or had he really had some kind of a spiritual encounter. He must pay more attention to his Guardian Angel and talk to him outside times of crisis, as that guy more than just hinted, that this may be the answer to many of lifes questions.

Small Town America

Speeding down Interstate 395 commerce speaks through the sound of the diesel engine and the hum of tyres of the big interstate trucks. The drivers whose attention may not waver even for a split second, as everyone moves in unison towards some distant destination. These giants of the highways travel with just one thought in mind, to be at their journeys end, and deliver safely and on time.

A little sign with an arrow pointing right unnoticed by the majority of travellers, says "Hangdog _ mile." Jimmy who at this stage has been behind the wheel of his big 12 wheeler artic truck for over 200 miles, feels the need for a comfort stop and something to eat. He swings his truck to the right and travels down the narrow road to Hangdog.

Hangdog, is no better or worse than any other small town or village off the beaten track. As America trundles by on 395, Hangdog with its potholed street and general air of neglect is a haven, where the long distance trucker is at least guaranteed at little peace and quietness, away from the noise and bustle of the highway. It consists of a Post Office and general store under one roof, with two pumps on the sidewalk, one gas and one diesel. A hundred or so clapboard houses, each with one or two wrecks of cars rusting away on these once landscaped lawns. Perhaps, a sign of a once more affluent past. A truck stop, that served a reasonably decent meal at not a very expensive price. Attached to the truck stop, a bar with a few casino machines, its best business done on Thursday, Welfare day. The mournful sound of the goods train hooter warns all of its approach, but never stops here. Right on the periphery of the town is a small neglected looking church, set in about half an acre of overgrown grass, shrubs, and tall old creaking trees. Headstones leaning over at different angles, and some that had fallen over entirely, were almost covered completely by the overgrown vegetation. A weather beaten notice board stood inside the locked gate, stating that, if the Pastor from the City was available there would be Divine Service on alternate Sundays. The times of the service were given, and also the Pastors name.

Like all other small towns Hangdog has its own resident whore, leaning invitingly and as provocatively as she dared, against a telegraph pole across from the general store. An uninterested mongrel comes along and pees against the pole. The dog and the whore sharing the same pole, each oblivious of the others presence, all they have in common is the telegraph pole. Each lacking ambition, circumstances the anchor that holds them both here.

Across the street MacTaggart the store owner comes out and brushes the stoop in front of the store. As he brushes he watches the whore as she waggles her crotch provocatively in his direction. Silently he thought, 'What I wouldn't give for just one hour a week with Belinda.' He would pay any money for this. Once last year he had two hours with Belinda in the barn back of his premises. His wife who had a bad bout of flu had taken some medication that completely knocked her out. Mac Taggart as one might say, took the bull by the horns and invited Belinda to the barn. It cost him $200.oo and in his opinion it was the best $200.oo he had ever spent in his entire life.

But now his ever vigilant spouse, as always on the ball, comes outside the store, took the brush and ushered Mac Taggart inside. As she looked across at the whore with a smirk on her face, Belinda gave her the two fingers, lit another cigarette and walked across to the diner. Here she might get a client from one of the truckers or one of the three or four guys travelling by cars.

Belinda perched herself on a high bar stool at the street end of the long bar come diner counter and ordered a beer. From here she could survey the whole premises. The two truckers also sitting at the counter were having a meal and chatting away as if they had known each other all their lives. More than likely they had never met before now, but, had the bond of the long distance trucking in common. There were six others, two couples, and two guys sitting apart and on their own. The Jukebox in the far corner was pumping out that country music hit by Tammy Wynette, "Stand by your man."

'Ah!' Thought Belinda, 'one of theses guys are a possibility.'

She turned slightly towards the older one of the two and showed her shapely legs and thighs, sure enough the older one sat up and took notice. Belinda finished her beer, put $2.oo on the counter, gave the guy that "Come on Honey." look of hers and left. Less than five minutes later here he was out and into his car, opened the passenger door, motioned Belinda in, and after a short discussion, drove a short distance to a secluded spot outside the town. Only the store keepers wife, who, as soon as Belinda left her perch at the pole, watched from the store window to see if Belinda would hook any of those inside. As the car left with Belinda and her client she felt a pang of jealousy. She did envy Belinda and her attractiveness to men, and also her capacity to make men happy. She couldn't even keep one man, her husband, happy. No one else in the town took any notice of the goings on around them. These lived by the premise of 'Live and let live.' After all Belinda was part of this very small community and in her own peculiar way a very necessary part of it. The county Sheriff Tom Parkes, had his office and jail 12 miles away, in a town would you believe, called Bethlehem. He would pay Hangdog a visit every day, believing his presence, was the deterrent which kept Hangdog crime free. Any decent criminal after taking one look at the town would know that, even on Welfare day the few dollars that would be floating around would only be a pittance. It would be just a big waste of time to hang around there. There wasn't a bank in the town, and the poker and pool players played for nickels and dimes. The Sheriff would stay for a short while, have a couple beers and mosey off again. Tom would turn a blind eye to Belinda and her trade. For this she gave him a free service a couple of times a week.

Probably in a few short years Hangdog would be just another ghost town, left to rot and disappear into oblivion. When someone died in Hangdog and the burial had taken place in the cemetery, a relative would go through the belongings of the deceased, take what was any good, and return to where they came from. Young couples didn't come here to set up home anymore. There was no school, no proper sewage system. Each house had its own what they called "The Bog House" at the bottom of their back garden. Only about half of the houses were occupied, and those that were occupied were nearly as derelict as the unoccupied ones. The nearest point of employment would be around 50 miles away in the city. The two truckers left the diner and returned to their trucks. Jimmy headed for 395 the other one climbed into the bunk built into the tractor unit, to have a few hours rest before travelling on.

After about an hour Belindas punter dropped her back into town and with a wave and a big smile went on his way. Belinda went into the bar and had a couple of beers, the dog lay quietly on a grain sack and basked in the evening sun. The lonely hoot of the train sounded as it approached, Mac Taggart was putting inside the shovels, rakes, and other tools from outside the store. Some of the elderly residents were gathering in the bar, to have a few beers and play cards. The evening sun was sinking in the west in a ball of fire. The solitary street lamp came on with a bit of effort, flickering on and off for 20 minutes before finally lighting fully. A dozen or so workers, from the surrounding farms came in, some just sat, had a beer and talked, the others joined the card school or played pool. This was the height of the social activity in Hangdog. Belinda from her perch at the end of the bar counter, weighed up the situation and knew that at least a couple of tricks could be turned here this evening. Outside another truck pulled in, the driver and a woman came in and sat at the counter. They both looked tired, after their meal they would more than likely settle down in the truck for the night. Hangdog though run down, and probably coming close to the end of its tenure, could still be a haven, and cater for those who choose to leave the highway for a little bit of peace and quietness.

Second Chance

Michael had become used to this each morning. Having breakfast in "Kylemore Café" in the Merchants Quay complex, had become a daily routine. He liked to relax here for awhile before going to his office. With a leisurely breakfast and a look through the 'Examiner' to keep abreast of the daily news, he felt this was a good way to start the day. As he walked towards the table area Michael was not prepared for the sight that met his eyes. 'Is it?' he thought and walked towards the girl sitting on her own. She looked in his direction as he approached, looked away, and then turned back quickly again.

"Michael?" she queried

"Liz is it really you?" He placed the tray on the table and sat heavily into the chair.

" My God! I don't believe this, after all these years." He said.

And his mind flashed back to the last day in February 10 years ago, almost to the day.

The curtain of his mind rolled up and images of that time passed through. He had never forgotten her and the years had not dimmed the memory of that first meeting. The way the years rolled by and no contact with her often made him despair. He had loved her from the first moment he had laid eyes on her and was never really able to get her out of his system.

Looking at her now he thought.

'How could it have happened? How could he have allowed it to happen? How could something that was so electric, so positive, come to such a quick and negative end?'

From the moment he had become aware of her presence in that packed auditorium 10 years ago he had not heard a single word spoken by the lecturer. Breathlessness filled his entire being. He thought, the pounding of his heart could be heard by everyone in that huge room and that his chest cavity would not be able to contain it. It was just going to burst out there and then. At that moment she looked in his direction and smiled, her lips parting slightly allowing her teeth to peek through. That took him completely off balance and he had the feeling of being suspended in mid air. The lecturer droned on and on, but Michael never heard another word.

He couldn't take his eyes off her and when the lecturer finished and the crowd dispersed he caught up with her in the quadrangle. He tipped her arm with his shaking hand and she turned to face him.

"Yes?" she said.

'My God she's beautiful.' His face reddened and suddenly he felt unsure of his ground. He wanted to apologise and walk away, but instead he took a deep breath and hesitantly he asked if she would have a coffee with him. She looked half smilingly at him, hesitated, and then said.

"O.K."

They went into the College canteen he ordered two coffees, and they sat at a table near the window. Sitting so close he was sure she could hear the thumping of his heart. He tried to make conversation, but his tongue seemed to be stuck to his pallet. Eventually he introduced himself, telling her his name was Michael O'Hanlon and he hoped to graduate next year in Commerce and Business studies.

The ice was broken and they filled each other in with their separate pedigrees. He was a farmers son from Co. Waterford, but not having much love for the land he left to further his education. He was into his last year at U.C.C., before heading out into the world to make his name.

Her name was Elizabeth Joyce but all her friends called her Liz. Her parents owned two hotels in the West of Ireland, -- one in Galway City, the other out in Connemara. She had graduated in accountancy and was finished with college, she was attending the lecture tonight because it was on business management, and this particular lecturer was tops in this field. Now that she had graduated she hoped like her parents, to find her niche in the hotel business. Although not returning to college she wouldn't be leaving Cork for another two or three weeks.

Michael asked if she lived in town, she said she did and that she shared a flat with three other girls up near St. Lukes cross. They finished their coffees and left the college. Walking with her to her bus stop on the Grand Parade he resisted the impulse to hold her hand. He asked if he could meet her again and after some hesitation on her part, an appointment was made to meet two evenings later.

On the appointed evening he stood at the statue near Mangans clock. While he waited he watched the corporation gardener renewing the plants in the nearby flower beds, a sure sign winter was over and spring was in the air. He looked at Fr. Mathews statue, a pigeon perched on his head. The statues head and shoulders bore witness to the fact that it was a favourite perching point for pigeons. The great apostle of temperance looking down on all and sundry was a grim reminder of less affluent days. As this point was also the city bus terminus he watched as the crews changed over. There was a little hut in the middle of the street known as the Fireman's rest that the busmen used for this purpose.

He could see Shandon in the distance its goldfish weather vane glistening in the evening sun, and thought of the old rhyme he had heard somewhere.

"Slightly coloured like its people, red and white is Shandon steeple."

He looked up at the very, very steep Patrick's Hill, from whose summit one had a wonderful panoramic view of the city. Looking down as far as where the street curved he could see the fine shops and limestone buildings. One would never have thought that at one time most of this side of Patrick Street had been burned to the ground. All of this formed the backdrop, to what he thought would be the happy start to the rest of his life.

Michael was getting anxious, they had made the meeting time for 3.30 it was now 4.15 and no sign of her. A strange feeling came over him, a kind of paranoia. Suddenly he felt that every passer-by glanced in his direction, and all had a smirky smile on their faces, knowing that he had been stood up. He felt like an actor on some huge stage with a brilliant spotlight .blotting everything out and leaving him the focus of everyone's attention. Even the pigeon perched atop Fr. Mathew's head seemed to look amusingly in his direction. For the umteenth time he looked at his watch, it was 4.35. By now the gardener had finished his chore and had moved on. He could feel the chill in the evening air and decided to leave. She was hardly going to turn up over an hour late.

As he walked along Patrick Street he remembered their parting on the Grand Parade two nights previous, and thought that the making of this appointment was only leading the fool further. She hadn't any intention of keeping it. Deep inside he did not want to believe this, even in that short space of time whatever passed between them could not have been all one sided.

For the next couple of weeks although he was very busy getting ready for his finals, he made some enquiries around college but to no avail. He found her apartment up in St. Lukes, but all the girl he met there could tell him was, that she arrived one evening took all her belongings, paid a months rent and told the landlord she wouldn't be returning. He hadn't the time to travel to Galway so he put the episode out of his mind as best he could until the exams were over.

Shortly after his graduation he went to the U.S. to spend a year with a computer firm in California. He had learned a lot there and enjoyed it so much that he stayed on for another two years. It is said, "That absence makes the heart grow fonder."

And in his case this was completely true. He could not get Liz out of his system, without her his life was unfulfilled. It was over four years since that night they had met in U.C.C. and he had walked her to the bus stop. He should have been well over her by now, after all it was even less than a one night stand, but his heart craved her now more than ever.

On coming back to Cork he set up his own computer business with an office on Camden Quay and a retail business around the corner on McCurtain Street. It went from strength to strength, and he had become a very respected member of the business community. But his mind kept harping back to Liz and he often wondered how she was doing. He resisted the temptation of going to look her up around Galway. She was probably settled down and happily married with a family by now. He didn't want to turn up like a ghost from the past, and anyhow she had more than likely put that part of her life well and truly behind her.

The years rolled quickly by and though he had a few liaisons, there was never anything serious.

Now sitting so close to her again his heart started to beat so fast he thought he would choke with emotion. He glanced at her hands, no wedding ring, could it be possible he was in with a second chance after all those years. After a little time just sitting and gazing and shaking her head in disbelief, Liz started to tell why she had not kept their appointment.

When she returned to her flat after leaving him that evening her brother was waiting for her. He had the bad news that her father had taken ill and was not expected to last the night. He would take her home to Galway straight away. Her father had not survived the night, and she was obliged to stay on and run the business with her mother who was shattered by her father's sudden and untimely death. After a week or so she returned to her flat in Cork to collect her belongings and has since been running the hotel out in Connemara.

She would be in Cork for the next week, as she would be attending a conference on tourism at the Silver Spring Hotel during the weekend. After that she would be taking a few days off before returning to Connemara. She had thought about him a lot during the years, and wondered what he must have thought of her when she hadn't kept their appointment. She apologised but there wasn't a thing she could do about it at the time.

Michael asked if she had married, and she answered "No"

He then asked if she had any commitment to anyone.

She said " No."

He then asked if she had some time to spare to day would she spend it with him.

"I have one or two things which I should look after, but I think now they can wait until tomorrow. This meeting must surely be a million to one chance, let's not tempt fate any further. My bags are locked in the booth of my car in the car park, so I'll just ring the hotel and let them know I may be a little late booking in"

Michael rang his office and told his secretary he would not be in at all to day. He was not to be contacted under any circumstances and anyhow as of now he was turning off his mobile phone. He then told Liz he had not married either. Up to now he had always lived in the hope that somewhere, somehow, their paths would meet again.

After breakfast they left the complex and walked hand in hand along

Patrick St. It was spring and the corporation man was just pulling up with his truck to renew the plants in the flower bed, the busmen were gathered around the little Fireman's Rest, Shandon was tolling out 11.00 o'clock, and Father Mathew's head was adorned with a pigeon.

Well Michael thought, 'What goes around comes around.' And felt that nothing and no one would ever part himself and Liz again. They would spend the rest of their lives making up those lost ten years.

Old Pals

Mick, Robert, and Steve, were very close friends, and one might say each a confirmed bachelor. Robert, better known as Bob or Bobby, tall and good looking with a nicely trimmed Clarke Gable moustache, balding a little and showing some grey. Looking at him one could be forgiven for thinking 'There goes the epitome of a gentleman.' Robert was the manager of a big supermarket. He was always impeccably dressed and never one to be seen outside his home without a nice shirt and tie. Even now though he was travelling he wouldn't be seen dressed casual. He was also a great hit with the ladies, but treaded very carefully when it looked some kind of a commitment was expected.

Mick, a furniture store salesman was always dressed to the nines as well. Of course it was part of their make up for the jobs they held. He was a bit over weight and was always threatening to trim down a bit. "I'm starting tomorrow." But it was always tomorrow, never today. Mick had no time whatsoever for women. If anyone broached the subject of some of the women joining their company, he would protest vehemently.

"Like Leeches" he would say. "All take and no give."

Steve, a bricklayer was the fittest one of the three, and had all the looks of a man that had spent his working life outdoors. In contrast he was usually dressed casually in jeans, open necked shirt and runners, as he now was, for the journey to Portugal. As regards women, he could take them or leave them. He was quite happy in their company or out side of it, but always on his guard just in case "Any of those hussies" thought he was fair game.

As well as their everyday work they were also musicians and it was the music that had brought them together many years ago. They formed a trio, with Steve on drums, Mick on piano accordion, Robert on saxophone and clarinet. They were very popular at weddings and other social gatherings as their repertoire consisted of a lot of old favourites. They played a great selection of Old Time Waltzes, Foxtrots, Military Two Steps, and some well known Dixieland standards. It wasn't like they had anything against women, they hadn't. But somehow true love never came their way. Each felt very happy with the set up as it stood, so why spoil a good thing. When looking at some of their work-mates and the stress they seemed to be under trying to make ends meet every week, they valued their freedom, and felt that was the way to go.

Everything went fine with the trio until it came to their annual holidays. Each year they would take off for a couple of weeks to some seaside town, book into a good hotel and relax. It wasn't easy to relax all the time, as Mick always seemed to have a crib. If it wasn't the food it would be the service, lighting in the bedroom, the bed was too hard, or not enough channels on the television. Of course the weather always got a bit of a knock. It was either too hot or too wet or too foggy. For Mick, it was never just right.

This year they had decided to go to the south of Portugal. There, to soak up the sunshine for two weeks.

Mick, was also a bit of a worrier, and didn't relish too much the thought of flying, especially since lately there had been a number of terrorist related incidents in different parts of the world. A number of these incidents had involved planes, and he got cold feet as soon as he entered the airport. He never mentioned these fears when they were making plans to go on their holiday, and in fairness he tried not to. But he just couldn't hold back.

"I'm not at all sure about this trip." He muttered.

And Steve hopped on him straight away.

"Do you know Mick you never lost it, always the same, having last minute doubts."

"Ah leave him alone Steve! You know he'll settle down once we get him on the plane. Won't you Mick?"

"Supposing there's terrorists on board? Fellas who are trained to drive planes, and before you could say "Jack Robinson" here we are heading for some foreign country. There to be imprisoned for a ransom and I ask you who would pay a ransom to have us released. They might decide to chop our heads off, or even worse, just because we're Irish."

"What did I tell yeh Bob? I told you leave him behind, not to bother to ask him along. God! Why are we always saddled with such a crank."

"Now Steve be nice, he can't help being the way he is. We'll go to the bar and get something to steady his nerves."

"Steady his nerves, sure all he drinks is orange juice and that acts on him so badly, that he's in and out of the toilet every five minutes."

"I'm not indeed, that only happens if I drink too much tea."

"Look Steve let's join the queue, get rid of our cases, and get our boarding passes, then we'll see what we can do about Mick."

"What to do about me is right. Don't talk as if I'm just a piece of luggage. Something that's to be thrown on the conveyor belt, weighed, labelled, and sent on its way.

"Now Mick, that's not the way it is at all. Don't take any notice of Steve, he's just looking for an excuse to go for a jar. If the truth were known Steve is just as nervous as you."

"I am not. Man I'd board an aircraft at the drop of a hat and fly anywhere. I'm a very experience flyer."

"Experienced my backside, the highest you ever flew was on the swings up in Fitzgerald's Park, the ones in Pipers out in Douglas went too high for you."

"That's very wrong Bob, didn't I fly to Dublin two years ago for the All Ireland Hurling final."

"Oh Yeh! And you got such a fright that you came home by train."

"And why? That plane was so small it should never have been allowed off the ground. Wasn't it you said to me that there was only a trainee pilot driving it and he hadn't even the proper uniform. He was dressed in jeans and a monkey hat. I'll never forget that trip I can assure you. There wasn't a puff of wind the same day and yet it was being blown all over the sky."

"O.K. O.K. Now stop all this goings on about the past, let's get our bags checked in and we'll go for a pint. We have more than an hour yet to boarding time."

After they check in and get their boarding passes they head for the bar. Steve calls.

"Two pints of Murphy's and a Club Orange."

Sitting in a secluded corner they talk about everything except the flight, trying to keep Mick's mind off the journey ahead. Then, over the P.A. system comes the announcement.

"We would like to announce that there will be a delay of one hour with Flight EI 106 to Lisbon. The flight crew, have been delayed by heavy traffic down town. We apologise for the inconvenience."

"Oh my God" Mick exclaimed "We're not in the plane yet and already there are problems. I knew it, and I said it all along, Ballybunion would be the best place for us. No one would listen to me, though. 'We'll take a foreign holiday both of you said', and here we are stranded in our own country. Even before we board there's problems. At least, we won't be hi-jacked here."

Robert stepped in straight away.

"Now Steve don't you say a word, and you Mick pull yourself together it's only one hour out of two weeks. We're fine and comfortable here, it's no big deal and it's not the end of the world."

"Not the end of the world; he says. Such a consolation, you sound like a prophet. Not the end of the world, indeed. What if it's not the crew? And as these people like to say it's just a technical problem, What then? Do you think they're going to tell us what's really wrong?"

Steve not able to shut up any longer turns on him.

"What the hell, if it is a technical problem, I'm sure they'll hardly take off until everything is right. And anyway, if you're born to be hung you won't be drowned, and if you're born to die in a plane, you'll go up in one. Another thing if your number's up there's not anything you can do about it."

"Oh yeh! What if the pilots number is up, What then? Does the plane land on its' own. Or maybe one of you guys would be able to land the thing? That's of course provided we're not flying over the ocean."

"Oh God! This is what it's going to be like until we get to Lisbon. Bob I told you leave him behind. He's driving us 'round the bend and we haven't the first pint finished yet."

"Excuse me, I've got to go to the Jacks."

"Well was I right or was I right? He hasn't two sips out of his orange juice and he's off to the toilet. We better check the boarding passes again, and make sure that Mick has an isle seat. Otherwise he'll be upsetting the whole plane, hopping in and out of the toilet."

"Oh for Gods sake Steve loosen up please, you're becoming a bigger pain in the butt that he is. As you well know we have the three seats near the window. We'll put Mick in the isle seat and if he is going to be running in and out to the toilet he won't disturb anyone. Now you lighten up a bit Steve, and relax."

"I suppose you're right Bob. But you know when Mick starts his capers I get a bit hyper, and I'm inclined to lose the head a bit. We'll have another pint and then we'll head for the boarding area. Here's Mick now, will you have another orange Mick?"

"No thanks Steve, I'll manage away with what I have. I met Jimmy Harris on my way back here, his wife is going away for two weeks with some of the women from work. I'd say he can't wait to get rid of her. Aren't we lucky we're not saddled with someone like her? A demon by all accounts."

"So I hear" said Bob "I believe a woman with a tongue like a rasp file. If we're on the same flight we'll just ignore her. If that's possible."

Finishing their drinks they head for the duty free and boarding area. Robert and Steve buy a bottle of Paddy and a bottle of Jameson, to have on hand when the reach their hotel. Beer and wine normally is cheap in Spain but the good spirits could be a bit expensive. Only about 15 minutes elapse when the girl at the boarding desk announces it is time to board the flight, and the three join the queue. Looking at Mick who is saying nothing but is shaking like a leaf, Steve is glad that Mick is not taking the bottles. He reckons Mick would have dropped them on the way out to the plane.

When their hand luggage is safely stowed in the overhead locker they take their seats. Steve near the window, Robert in the middle, and Mick in the isle seat. When everyone is on board and all the safety belts are checked the plane moves slowly towards the runway. By the time the stewardess finishes reading the safety instructions the plane is ready for takeoff. As the plane roars down the runway, Robert notices that Mick is shaking like mad, and is looking up to heaven and he looked to be praying hard. He doesn't say anything to Steve who is looking out the window, seemingly oblivious of everything except the flashing by green fields and houses below. After a few minutes the plane levels off and a sigh of relief from Mick, who immediately opens his safety belt and goes quickly down the isle to the toilet. Robert looks at Steve who has a smug "Well what did I tell you?" smile on his face, but when Mick does return he doesn't say anything. Then the three settle down, hopefully for an uneventful journey to Portugal.

On the Buses.

Mistaken Identity.

During the summer I went to Shannon Airport to pick up some American visitors and transfer them to Jurys Hotel, Limerick. When the transfer was made two people would be staying on board as these were going to Lisdoonvarna. As I thought this sounded straight forward enough. Along with myself on the coach was a lady courier, she made sure all the passengers were here and the luggage was stowed safely underneath. A special seat up front is provided for the courier, so we were chatting as we headed out of Shannon.

As we came on to the main limerick road A voice directly behind me said,

"That sure is a good looking driver Marge."

Marge answered. "Sure is Chuck."

The hair on the back of my neck prickled a little and my face reddened some. I look at the courier, she smiled and winked at me, and said.

" You've got a live one there Pat."

Now I've been told I'm a good driver, I've been told I'm an awful driver, some say I drive too fast, some say I drive too slow, but, no one ever said until now that I was a good looking driver. As this was only a transfer from airport to hotel the courier wasn't commentating as she normally would if we had been out on tour. Just as we were passing Bunratty Castle the same voice sounded again.

"That driver sure is good looking Marge"

"You're right on there Chuck."

The courier smiled again, but I was beginning to feel a little uncomfortable to say the least. I thought to myself 'I hope this guy doesn't fancy me.' Tour coach driving is taxing enough without having to put up with someone like him. In our job there is nothing worse than trying to put up with a randy male or female tourist. In any case I would be finishing with him in ten or fifteen minutes when we would reach Jurys. As we were approaching Jurys that dreaded voice sounded again.

" Marge, that sure is the best looking bus driver I've ever seen."
And Marge probably getting a little annoyed at this stage, tells him.

" O.K., Chuck, but put a zipper on it will ya."
On arriving at Jurys we discharge our passengers and the courier says she will book them in, and as there was only two passengers going to Lisdoonvarna I could carry on, on my own. Then she told me the two for Lisdoon were Chuck and Marge.

"Chuck and Marge" I exclaimed "I hope you're codding me." But, she wasn't.

I thought to myself 'What kind of capers a guy like chuck would be getting up to in Lisdoonvarna a place noted for its frivolities. I would also be overnighting in Lisdoon as I was picking up a tour at the Hydro hotel next morning. I hoped that Chuck and Marge would not be joining this tour.

Well! I needn't have worried. As we left Jurys car park, got on to the main road, and headed for Lisdoon, I heard a loud exclamation behind me.

" Oh no! God dammit Marge, I thought she was the driver."
Moral of the story?
" Never take the book by the cover."

A Randy Lady.

One morning travelling south through Kildare County, I was telling the people about the racecourses, the thoroughbreds, and the Stud Farms for which the county is famous.

"As a matter of fact" I said, "Some of the finest studs in the country are located here in Kildare."

From about half down the coach a ladys voice was heard to exclaim,

"Pat, do you think we could pull over for an hour."

Vesilinca.

Then there was the guide from Sweden, who, no matter how many times I sat down with her and said, "Magillacuddy Reeks, Magillacuddy Reeks," She could not get it right. When we were stopped at Aghadoe Heights viewing the mountains and lakes, she would tell them about how Irelands highest mountain Carrantwohill was located in the range across the lake known as the Macuddagilly Reeks. She just couldn't get it right. I don't think the passengers ever noticed.

Delilah.

Well, my friends, after two weeks on the road all that's left for me to say is "Thank you." Thank you for visiting our country and I sincerely hope you enjoyed the experience. Thank you for travelling Cronins' Coaches, we are not the cheapest, but we are the best. Thank you for being so nice to myself and Delilah. I have worked with Delilah on numerous occasions and have always found her to be the epitome of what a tour guide should be.

She has always performed away and above the call of duty. Sitting here alongside me I can see she's blushing because of the well deserved praise I'm heaping upon her. As you well know my friends you must praise the bridge as you cross it.

She is not what our late President Éammon De Valera might call a " Comely Irish Maiden" who may be found dancing at the cross roads on a fine summers evening, and as she would say herself her speech is sometimes a little articulated.

There were a few incidents here and there where she may have got gotten a bit mixed up. Like when Patrick Sarsfield and not Patrick Pearse was the one that read the Proclamation from the top of the G.P.O. on Easter weekend 1916. How Gerry Adams was knighted by the Queen for being such a good ambassador abroad for the United Kingdom. Can you remember when we came to he Cliffs of Moher, how she was at pains to make sure that if anyone of you did fall over that you would be sure to look South as the it was a much nicer view.

When she was explaining about the Phoenix park and the Duke of Ormonde who opened the park in 1692 and he was the one who introduced the herd of deer to the Phoenix Park, and how their ancestors were still roaming freely there. I'm sure you will not hold these little slip ups against her. And when it comes to the final farewells at Shannon, and you the decent American people that you are will not be found wanting when it comes to showing your appreciation, for the wonderful tour of our country Delilah has given us. So may I on behalf of Delilah and myself may I wish you a safe journey home to you family and friends.

"Slán agus beannacht Déi oraibh go Léir."

Papal Blessing.

A number of years ago my first trip to Rome was almost a disaster. Really there was nothing almost about it. It was a disaster. From the time we left Cork things started happening. We had 40 people. Our first stop was Waterford and some at the back of the coach complained that the emergency door was could not be opened if there was an emergency. This was on account of the false floor that had been fitted in order to get in two extra seats.

When we got to Rosslare we picked up our two guides, an Irish guy and an Italian girl. Fortunately I was the one who found them as the Irish guy smelled like Cork Distillery and to say the least was a bit unsteady on his feet. Fortunately I got him straight into his cabin without anybody on the coach being aware of his condition. After a few hours on board the ferry he surfaced and I introduced him to the people.

I am not going to go into any more details about that trip now, as there is some other one, who tells me he's writing a book about it. So I'll let it to him.

Except this one incident which happened to me personally in the Vatican. We were attending the Mass by the Holy Father Pope John Paul 11. As I had to park the coach in a designated parking area I was later than the others getting in. Now when I did get in the rest of the people had gone right up as near to the altar as they could. From the altar rails to beyond where I was standing a brass rail ran around in a semi-circle. I spotted that inside this rail was a stairway leading down to the next floor level, so I thought,

'You know, when the Pope has finished Mass, it's quite possible that he would come this way and down these stairs'.

I decided I would take my chances and stay here during the mass.

I was standing here for a short while when who comes in and stands alongside of me but Mother Therese of Calcutta. I looked at her and she smiled and said "Bonjourna" of course in my best Italian I said "Bonjourna Mother Therese." She muttered something else that I didn't catch so I just shook her hand. Anyway when Mass was finished sure enough the Pope came down in our direction and as he was passing gave a big smile and a nod in our direction. Of course we smiled back, he blessed us, and went on down the stairs. While he was disrobing with the help of the now Bishop John Magee, the Pope turned to John Magee and said.

"John should I know that little nun out there who was standing along side Pat McCarthy."

Ikey

Ikey was small for his 11 years and sported a big unruly mop of sandy coloured hair. He was usually dressed in denim shirt, tattered pullover, faded jeans, and boots that were at least one size too large, but which hid his badly holed socks. His height didn't trouble him too much. What troubled Ikey more was his surroundings and that awful name. How he hated that name, and he never knew why people called him that. He knew he was different, and he felt he didn't need a lot of height to realise this. People told him his surroundings were part of his culture, yet, what kind of culture was it that kept him and his family in such dirt and squalor.

He was christened William Oliver but his mother was the only one who ever called him William. Sometimes she called him Billy. He liked Billy he thought there was a manly ring about it. Being of the Itinerant class they had always lived on the side of the road, travelling around the country from the outskirts of one town to the outskirts of another. Never being allowed to park too near any town.

Ikey liked the caravan it was a fine large vehicle with plenty of room for his parents and himself. It was its location that always left a lot to be desired. His father always tried to make sure that he parked on ground that would be a couple of feet above the level of the road. This didn't always save them. If the weather was really bad and a drain further along the road would get clogged up, water and mud would swirl around the caravan, too near for comfort. God! How he hated this. It made him wonder if this was going to be his lot forever, or was he, like his three elder brothers, also destined for the building sites of England. However, he didn't think the buildings sites could be any worse than this.

His brothers, Tom 24, Martin 22, and Patrick 19 went off to England and worked on the building sites somewhere around London. They never as far as Ikey knew sent home money to help their parents. When they came home last Christmas, they were like strangers to Ikey. They each gave him a few pounds, and then took off to see their friends and have a good time. They hardly stayed in the caravan at all while they were at home, which really suited Ikey. After two weeks they returned to England and Ikey was glad to see the back of them, as he felt he had more control over his own situation when it was just him and his parents.

Elizabeth his only sister the eldest of the family, a beautiful girl had met and married a very nice Galway man, Fintan Joyce. They had two children a boy age six and a girl aged three, the stamp of herself. When she came to visit them it was great. Ikey admired Elizabeth she never denied heritage. She was thankful that she had risen above it. Ikey hoped that some day he would also rise above it, and become part of a wider and more affluent community. His mother doted over those two kids. Her sincere wish was, to settle near Galway, and hoped to be part of their growing up. A little house in Galway would surely be wonderful.

He sometimes thought about his mother, a very religious woman, and how her spirit seemed to remain unbroken. How she kept soldiering on in spite of everything. She had a great devotion to the Sacred Heart, whose picture was so placed that you saw it immediately you entered the caravan. This was a picture that gazed at you silently no matter where you stood, and it was never without a lighted night light in front of it. The holy water font hanging just inside the door was never allowed to run dry. His mother always had the kind word and wouldn't pass judgement on anyone. Whenever a nasty comment was made about someone she would say,

"Let the Lord be the judge, as He will have the last word in any case."

She was resigned to her lot, and hoped for better deal when she passed on from this world. She was a tall woman and looked every one of her 51years, her once beautiful face was now criss crossed with the ravages of time. A woman who, though, had plenty to do around the caravan would often give a day thinning turnips, mangolds, or other root crops for some farmer.

His father, a big strong man, balding, with bushy eye brows, and most of the time in need of a shave. Being unshaven and the bushy eye brows gave him a very stern look. He was really a very quiet man and in his own peculiar way also very spiritual. Though life was tough Ikey never heard him complain. He had his own pick-up truck. This vehicle was used to tow the caravan, and also used it for his business of buying and selling scrap. He would leave the caravan each morning around 8.00 o'clock and return at lunchtime with a load of scrap. He would tip the load near the caravan, have his lunch and spend the evening away collecting more. It wasn't a great way of making a living but along with the dole they were able to survive.

Ikey wasn't at all sure what class or culture he belonged to. Some said he was a Traveller, others said he was an Itinerant, there were those who called him a knacker, and those who called him a Tinker or a Pavee. He like Tinker best, as to him it seemed to be nearer his so-called culture. He remembered being told at one time that the tinkers were forced to leave their homes and smallholdings mostly during the Great Famine. The English landlords who owned most of land got them evicted, and put them out on the roadside, and their little thatched cottages were burned to the ground. Trying to keep body, soul, and family together they learned quickly the craft of the tinsmith. These craftsmen travelled around the country making buckets, pots, pans, and showed great skill in repairing milk churns and other farm and kitchen utensils. These were honest people who worked their way around the country, never looking for charity, and always ready to work to keep the wolf from the door.

Another thing Ikey hated was going to the shop in the local town for whatever his mother would require, be it groceries or other messages. He would love to have wandered around the shop and gaze at all it held. Along with groceries there were sweets and lollipops, bill-hooks, slashers, shovels, buckets, rakes, and such a conglomeration of other goods that it was impossible to take it all in at a glance. These shops were usually split in two, a pub on one side and the shop on the other. Over all this, hung the unmistakable smell of porter and paraffin oil. Where Ikey was concerned this was the icing on the cake, it gave the place a character all it's own. He had once read a book called "Aladdin" and these shops always reminded him of that story. This was his Aladdin's cave.

Ikey never got the chance to linger for long. He would be just inside the door when all those in the shop turned to look at him as if he was trespassing, and irrespective of how many were in the shop he would be served first and sent on his way. Often he would think 'Why is my money alright but not me?' In every town it was the same and it took him some time before he understood why this always happened. When it did hit he felt so hurt, because honesty and consideration for others had always been a priority of his mothers teaching. .

He never talked a lot, but listened to his parents and others in such a quiet and unobstrusive way, that all issues big and small were discussed in his presence. He had the knack of being there without being noticed.

Ikey had secret ambitions, he didn't want to spend his life roaming from one place to another. To do this he had to go to a regular school. Up to now his education had been, to say the least, a little haphazard, never being stationary long enough to catch up. All the different schools he had attended meant for him that there had been no continuity. Now, all this looked like changing for a while at least.

A priest and a lady from some school board of management called one evening to discuss the receiving of his confirmation. His parents agreed that this was a most important sacrament and would co-operate in every possible way. Then and there arrangements were made for the caravan to be sited on a hard stand at a halting site near Cork. From the following Monday he would attend the special school for travellers children. Ikey liked the halting site, with its concrete stand for the caravan. It was kept nice and clean, with running water, toilets, showers, electric hook up points, and a rubbish skip. But, one of the most important things for Ikey was that he didn't have to trudge through three or four inches of mud every time he stepped outside.

He would dearly love to live in a house, but to him the halting site was the next best thing. Here he would have other kids to play with and from here he would be able to attend school full time. He loved the thought of going to school, meeting other children and picking up on his reading and writing. Of course going to school meant that he would be always dressed in the best clothes available, his mother would see to that.

He didn't have many books. Those he did have, a woman who visited the caravan periodically had brought them. She must be from some charity or other, as she also brought some second hand clothes. Among the books were some adventure books, such as "Treasure Island" "Robinson Crusoe" and "Huckleberry Finn." He liked Huckleberry Finn the best, Ikey felt he could identify somewhat with him. He would love to have been part of his adventures on the river, but also he wished he could have friends like those of Huckleberry Finn.

On Monday morning all spruced up and with a few school books in his satchel, he boarded the bus. This was a special bus that took him and other children from the halting site to school on the other side of the city. For Ikey this was the start of a new adventure. As they left the north side of the city he felt like Huckleberry Finn, pushing the raft out from the landing stage on the river, and wondering what new sights and experiences lay before him.

Travelling along the top of Churchfield he looked down on the city of Cork and remembered a line from a song he had heard his mother singing, "Beautiful city my home by the Lee." He wondered how many people lived in Cork, as the houses seemed to stretch out for miles in all directions. Going down Fair Hill he watched other children chatting happily on their way to school. Obviously, judging by their neat uniform, a different school to him. As the bus travelled down this very steep hill he could see straight out through the front windscreen. The city spread out before him. He could see lots of houses, large buildings, many spires, a very high square towered building with a golden fish on top and huge clocks on both sides that faced them. Stopping at traffic lights for a minute and ignoring the chatter of the other children, Ikey gazed at the magnificent church in front of them. Surely this awesome building must be a cathedral, he would ask the bus driver when he got to know him better. They passed this great church still going down hill when suddenly the River Lee comes into view. He didn't expect it to be so wide, and the water was so near the top of its walls.

The bus wound its way around a few narrow streets to a very wide street. The traffic was so heavy that Ikey feared they would never get through. Eventually they did, and came to a bridge crossing the river. As he looked out the window he wondered if Hucks' river was as beautiful and as fast flowing as this one. A short distance further on they crossed over another river, so he decided Cork must have two rivers, something else he must ask the driver about. Turning left along the quayside he could not believe his eyes, -- Ships. Ikey had seen ships before but never at such close quarters. Some were discharging their cargo and some were loading out. He wondered where in the world they had come from, what goods they were transporting, and when discharged or loaded where they would be sailing to.

They passed this area quickly and travelled on through a residential district. Here each house was large, had a lovely lawn sloping down to the road, and the lawns were dotted here and there with fine trees and shrubs. On a little further and another set of traffic lights, he marvelled at the number of sets of traffic lights they encountered. It was great when they stopped at these as it gave him some extra time to take in his surroundings.

Leaving the residential area they came by the river again, now much wider, and a little harbour with its fishing boats pulled up on a concrete ramp that sloped up from the river. Strewn along the quayside he could see the fishing nets and the fishermen inspecting them before putting them back on the boats. Then, suddenly comes into view this magnificent castle with its turreted towers, its wrought iron gates, and the river lapping its rocky foundations. Ikey had never seen anything like this before. This must surely be the home of a Prince and Princess, or maybe a King and Queen.

They drove around the waters edge and he looked across at the far side. He decided that not even Huckleberry Finns' river was as grand as this. There and then he vowed that some day he would really explore it right down to the sea, where he knew every river ended. Never in his wildest dreams did Ikey believe that such wonders would ever be his to behold. His heart was beating uncontrollably, and as the bus entered the schoolyard he slowly returned to normality.

A young woman came to meet them off the bus, and asked the driver if everything was O.K. She then looked for William Farrell and Ikey stepped forward, she put her hand on his shoulder and guided him towards the classroom. She said her name was Therese and she was his class teacher. Therese was tall, dressed in blue jeans, denim shirt, with her long fair hair tied up in a pony tail. She was young enough to be his sister.

There were a number of other kids already in the classroom when he and his fellow travellers arrived. Therese brought him to the front of the class and introduced him to the others. They all stood up and with one voice said "Welcome William." This made him feel so good. She then showed him to the seat and desk that he would occupy from now on.

What with learning, making new friends, and playing in the spacious yard, before he knew it the day was over and the bus was back. It was time to return home. On leaving the school - yard the bus took a left turn, and Ikey realised they would be returning home by another route. So, this day's adventures were not over yet. On the return journey they passed through roundabouts and dual carriages ways until they came to the city, and again crossed over the two rivers. They passed grand buildings, many churches, and again the square towered one with the clocks and the golden fish weather vane. Some day he would sit near the driver and ask about all of these.

When they reached the halting site each thanked the driver and said they would see him in the morning, and he drove away smiling broadly. Ikey rushed in the caravan door, and on seeing him his mothers' eyes lit up with welcome and delight. She sat him down beside her and said, "Well William tell me all about your day."

He recounted every detail and a tear came as she listened in awe. She couldn't believe that such a small lad could take in so much in one day. She felt so proud of him and felt that here was one who would not waste his education time.

A little later looking up from his homework he watched as his mother prepared dinner. He thought how hard it must be for her to have a hot meal for them each evening. Even though the caravan was large the facilities for washing and cooking were very basic. When not on the halting site, water had to be drawn, from somewhere in two large churns which were kept outside the caravan. This was a job himself and his father had to do every second evening when parked on the roadside. The stove on which his mother cooked had only two rings and was fired by sticks and turf, yet she always seemed to manage and come up with a really good meal.

When his father arrived later on, the three of them sat down to dinner, and his father who hardly ever seemed to notice him said, "Tell me Billy my boy how did you get on to day?"

'Billy! he called me Billy.' He was so overcome with emotion that he was unable to answer straight away. What a day this had been. An adventure, and he hoped with much more to come, that even Huckleberry Finn could not match, and on top of all that, it looked as if he may have lost that horrible name.

The Rosary Beads

I can never remember going out our front door without first dipping my finger in the holy water font hanging on the wall, making the sign of the cross, reciting a short prayer and asking the Lords help and guidance for the day. This custom was inherited from my mother who told us the gesture would protect us from all evil while we were away from the home. It had the power to keep the devil at bay at all times. Like a lot of mothers of that period, after the second World War, she had a faith that could literally move mountains, and I'm sure it often did. She would also be the one to insure that the holy water font never ran dry.

But more so etched in my memory is the Rosary beads that hung alongside. This was an old family heirloom passed down from her grandmother, to her mother, and to herself. There was nothing spectacular about it. It wasn't one of those fine flashy beads made from mother of pearl, crystal, or some other grand material. It didn't shine it didn't sparkle, it was a plain old brown well worn rosary.

Perhaps at one time it was red or green or white and the intervening years had taken its toll on its colour as well. The beads were of little wooden balls woven on a light wire that showed the many repairs that had been made here and there to it over the years. Also the beads were no longer round, they had become oval shaped from constant use.

The crucifix was of wood, the figure a sort of dull metal whose features like the beads were worn almost smooth.

Yet it conveyed something of the faith of our ancestors, of generations gone. Though it just hung there, it had an aura all its own, and if one lingered awhile one could feel an energy emanating from it, that gave one a really good feeling for the rest of the day.

It was a line to the past. One was reminded of times when in most homes in the parish, the family would gather each evening around that all seeing Sacred Heart picture, that also looked as if it had been in the family for generations, and recite the family rosary.

Countless rosaries were said on its beads as fingers slid effortlessly along their surface, to storm heaven with the petitions of family, friends, and neighbours. It was an engine of ceaseless prayer from start to finish. It was part of the fabric of the family, and each member had a great respect for its powerful prayer. One could feel a spiritual uplifting by its presence alone just hanging there on the wall, an acknowledgement that the old folk really knew what life was all about. These people had such a blind faith in its constant use, they had no fear of death. Although not well educated, when it came to the crunch they showed a great knowledge of spiritual things, and in their wisdom lived their lives in complete cohesion with God. For them the road to eternity was paved with love, honesty, and prayer, and none more powerful than the rosary.

Mike

Once upon a time there was a boy named Mike. Mike was a dreamer. Not in the lazy sense, but in a way that he could give license to his imagination and let it run riot in whatever direction it cared to take. He could sit and brood for long periods, and from the sights and sounds around him draw vivid pictures in his mind. People called him dizzy but he didn't mind this at all. He knew one had to be a little dizzy, to be part of the strange adventures that he found himself taking part in. He loved to listen to his father, who was from a very remote area of West Kerry, recount tales of Pishógs, Leprecahuns, Banshees, and other strange creatures that inhabited the place of his boyhood.

When it was holiday time from school his parents rented a cottage on a mountainside not far from Killorglin town. While on holidays here, his brothers, his sisters, and himself would roam the nearby meadows and hills each day in search of adventure, and it was Mike who always led the pack. He could persuade the others that they were an ancient nomadic tribe dressed in animal skins, and like the American Indian the whole country - side was their domain. Mike had a way about him that transported them in such a manner that made them believe they were from another era or if necessary from another dimension.

Even though they were city kids they loved the few weeks spent in the country each year. Mike being the eldest they all looked up to him, and during these ramblings around the countryside they treated him like their chief.

When he said stop and asked for quietness, they would stop and not utter a word. Then Mike would point out something unusual he had spotted. It might be only an outcrop of rocks, it might be a tree, although of the same species as all the other trees around, would have some unusual feature. It could be growing at a different angle or, he would point to where ivy had taken root at the trees' base, and how eventually this would strangle and kill the tree.

Mike also seemed to have a sixth sense. Suddenly he would motion all to be quiet, and he would show them some animal that would be quite unaware of their presence. It might be a fox, a hare, a rabbit, a weasel, a stoat, a rat, or even a young deer. Whatever it was they would sit there quietly and observe, as it went about its daily business. Mike would talk very lowly giving a commentary on the animals' behaviour. So every day they learned something about animals, birds, flowers, heather, trees, and insects. There was an abundance of all of these on this mountain, and Mike possessed a good knowledge of each.

One day while crossing a field, where the new mown hay was laid out in swathes, a whirlwind whipped up. It travelled across the field lifting pieces of hay as it went. Mike bade the others to be quiet and observe as he told them.

"This wind that lifts the hay so gently, is known as a Shee Gaoithe or Fairy Wind."

He then explained that the fairies in Ireland do not have wings and this is how they travel from one location to another.

The others watched in awe as the whirlwind blew on its way, with wisps of hay caught up and went whirling along with it. When it stopped a few fields away the hay fell gently to the ground. The kids had watched wide eyed, believing they could see the fairies hanging on to the wisps of hay as it travelled along.

In the evening they would return to the cottage tired and hungry. Almost as soon as they had eaten, one by one they would slip away to bed. That is, all except Mike.

On the fine summer evenings just as darkness was falling Mike would go to his favourite place. This was a very large lump of granite rock about five or six feet high. On this he would sit, observe, and listen. From here, he could see in the twilight right across the valley. The shapes of trees, ditches, and farmhouses would transform before his very eyes and become strange objects. The trees would take on shapes like Sailing Ships sailing on a hedge row sea, of high buildings like those he had seen in pictures of New York, or, even Camels trekking across the desert. All this would conjure up into a huge panoramic landscape viewed by him alone.

He listened to the sounds of the night. The swish and slurp of the cows tongues as they grazed in the nearby fields. The snort of a horse and the sound of its hooves, as it moved from one field to another. The bleat of a sheep as it called to its lambs. The restlessness of the crows in the high trees that surrounded the cottage, the wood pigeons who seemed to be forever flapping their wings and never stopped cooing. He could hear the sound of small animals scurrying around in the night, and sometimes, he would hear the terrified scream of a rabbit caught in a snare.

Looking up at the sky he would pick out the 'Plough,' the 'Big Dipper, the outline of 'Leo,' the 'Milky Way,' the Great Bear,' the 'Little Bear,' and of course the brightest of all the 'North Star.' He marvelled at the shooting stars as they sped across the sky on their way to oblivion, "Another soul gone to Heaven," his grandmother used to say. He would become so absorbed in his surroundings he felt he was the only one left on earth, and all this was his alone.

Then, one night it happened, Mike heard the singing. It was coming from a corner of the field where there was a Rath or a Fairy Fort. This Fairy Fort was covered in scrub and large bushes, such as Blackthorn, Whitethorn, Fuchsia, Thistles and other wild plants. Although it was really spoiling the field for agricultural purposes, the owner of the land would never run a plough or harrow too close to it. It was said that if this ever happened, this particular field would never again yield a crop of any sort. The Fairies would have their revenge.

The voice sang "With me tick-a-tack-tick-tack-too, tick-a-tack-tick-tack-too, all my life I'll be happy just mending the fairy shoe."

Sliding down from his rock Mike went towards the sound of the singing. There wasn't a light as such, but the area was bathed in a kind of fluorescent glow. In this glow Mike saw a very small person dressed in green baggy suit, buckled shoes, and a funny looking hat. He was sitting on a three legged stool and mending what Mike took to be a very small shoe. Mike recognised him straight away as a Leprechaun, and he was so engrossed in his work that he hadn't noticed Mike as he stole slowly and silently towards him. Mike shot out his hand and grabbed him. Well! The Leprechaun left out such a roar that Mike nearly dropped him. He started yelling.

"Let me go, let me go, it's lies all lies, I don't have a pot of gold."

He wriggled and shouted some more, then cooling down a bit, he whimpered.

" I'm just a poor Leprechaun trying to earn my keep mending the shoes of the Fairies."

Without easing his grip Mike looked at him and said,

"I don't want your pot of gold. I honestly don't. Although I've often wished I would meet a Leprechaun I didn't believe I ever would. Now that I have do you think we could be friends? I would like for us to talk awhile, and I promise that whatever passes between us this night will be strictly our secret."

The Leprechaun peeked from under his funny hat, which by now had gone somewhat askew on his head, and said,

"My name is Patrick and I live with the Fairies in the fort beneath us, but! I do have my own pad down there. You're not the first human I've seen, but you are the first that has caught me, and that I've spoken to. I do have some mystic powers and since you don't want my pot of gold, of which I don't have any, I may be able to grant you a wish or two."

"That's great" Said Mike "There's one thing I would like very much and that is to visit your Fairy fort. I've often wondered what it's like down there."

"No problem" said Patrick a wry smile on his face. "Let me down I'll collect up my gear and we'll be on our way."

But Mike wasn't having any of this.

"Listen Patrick I'm not a fool or an idiot you know. If I let you down you'll scamper away and I'll never see you again."

Patrick lowered his head and looked hurt. "I thought we were friends."

Mike said; "I'm sorry for not trusting you, but I've heard too many tales about Leprechauns escaping from their captors."

"I can't go and let my tools behind. Someone might come along and steal them"

"I don't care." said Mike "I'm not letting go of you"

Then Patrick looking cunningly around him exclaimed,

"Hark! Listen! What's that sound I hear?" And pointing up the field he said, "Is that your Mother I hear calling you?"

Mike turned to where the Leprechaun had pointed, and looked up the field towards the cottage. He didn't see anything or hear anything and when he turned back to Patrick, the light had gone, the Leprechaun had gone, and he was left sitting all alone on his rock. Mike thought to himself 'had the whole thing been a dream?' He found it hard to believe that he had imagined it all. What if it had been real, and what if he had caught a Leprechaun? Then he laughed to himself, my God if it was real how easily he had been fooled, and he was sure as in that lovely poem "The Leprechaun" by W.P.Joyce, "The Fairy was laughing too."

The Homecoming

Well Helen, this is it, he's flying in this morning. In one way I'm dreading our meeting and yet I'm looking forward to his arrival as well. I wonder what he looks like after 23yrs? 23yrs! That makes him 44. Did I ever think I'd see the day, when I would have a son 44yrs old, and now that day has come.

God! the day he left home for Australia is still etched in my memory as if it were only yesterday. At the time I thought he was gone forever never to see him again, and I wasn't far wrong, was I? There's a lot of water gone under the bridge in that time, with many changes to home, family and country. You Helen, God rest you today, in that motherly instinct of yours, sensed, that on this earth you two would never meet again, and his leaving broke your heart. That morning you were inconsolable. What's that you said to me when we left him at Shannon and headed for home? I'm trying to think. Oh yes!

You said. "It's the beginning of the end Jim. The others are bound to follow, when one goes all go. Soon we'll be two old people getting in each others way around the house."

It wasn't quite like that though. The rest didn't emigrate. Our one daughter Michelle, and our two other sons Tim and Donald, married and settled not too far from the old home. Wasn't it great when you were alive Helen and their visits were regular, how you loved to see them, and as time went by, their children. Our grandchildren how they loved you, how they cried at their loss when you passed away, and Mary our eldest granddaughter sang the "Ave Maria" so beautifully as we walked slowly behind you down the Isle and followed you out to your final resting place at Kilcully.

Then things changed somewhat. Your death left such an incredible vacuum in the home. I couldn't blame them for their irregular visits after that. As you well know Helen I'm not the best host or socialiser in the world. Only you seemed to understand this, and you always covered well for me when the occasion arose. Much as I loved them I couldn't really handle them when they came to visit. The last 5yrs have been hard Helen. I'm really only just surviving without you.

You remember Helen after he left for Australia how we reminisced about the past and agreed that James always had a restless spirit. He could never settle down at home. The books he read, the long walks he took, the way he'd suddenly pack his bag, hop on a bus or train, and not return for a few days. Even the job as a long distance truck driver he had on the last two years he was at home, kept him away for days, and sometimes weeks at the time. We really shouldn't have been all that surprised that he took off for the other side of the world. He was adventurous and wanted to fly, and when he did spread his wings, he really put some distance between us.

Helen, can you ever forget the time he was learning to play the Banjo? It nearly drove the two of us around the bend, and just as he was beginning to master it he threw it to one side and didn't bother with it anymore.

I suppose you could say he was good enough at school, but harboured a great dislike for some of his teachers. His love of Irish history and the Irish language was amazing for someone who found it so hard to pin himself down to any one thing. Remember his girlfriends Helen? These came and went like the weather. He was a bit of a Romeo alright. He never stayed long with any of them. He was never one to commit himself to a long term relationship. As he said when you asked him about all these lovely girls that came in and out of his life,

"Mam I like to play the field, I'm not ready to settle down just yet."   The fact that he never married at all might be a stroke of luck just now, at least he's arriving home without any excess baggage.

I'm heading for the Airport now Helen to pick him up and bring him home. I've already phoned about his flight and it's due on time. He wrote to tell me he hopes to get a job as a coach driver with one of the local coaching firms, so you see Helen, he's still somewhat restless. He hasn't mentioned anything about returning to Australia, so I'm hoping he'll be around for some time. Although no one can ever replace you, it would be nice to have a bit of company around the house again. It gets so lonely, especially at night.

Helen, pray for us, that after all these years of little or no communication we'll hit it off. Oh how I wish you were here, it would be so much easier. I'll talk to you again tonight and let you know how things are with us. Love you.

The Meeting

Dearest Helen just to let you know James is home safe and sound, and it's well he's looking. He really looks great, very fit looking and tanned. At first I wondered if he had changed much and if I would recognise him. I was going to hold up a card with his name on it, but Helen there was no need. As he came out of the arrivals area I knew him straight away, and him me.

As he came towards me he dropped his case and carrier bag, Helen I thought I would die there and then with the mighty hug he gave me. The tears flowed freely from both of us. Oh God Helen! How I wished you were here. Although it's 23 years and he's travelled thousands of miles he's still, as always, travelling light. Just one suitcase, not a very large one, and a small carrier bag.

Not much was said until we got to the car. His first words were, "I'd like to visit Mams grave before going home."

I was delighted and overwhelmed by this. And you Helen what about you? I'm sure you were so happy when you saw him there. The words from the song "Danny Boy" came to mind,

"I will hear how soft you thread above me,

And o'er my grave will warmer, sweeter be."

He knelt and was very silent for a few minutes then he got up and looked at me with tear stained eyes, shook his shoulders and spread his arms in a gesture of hopelessness. As we walked silently back to the car I believe his heart was breaking, he was probably wishing he could turn back the clock, and embrace you and tell you how much he loved and missed you.

On arriving home Michelle was there with her youngest daughter Lauren, and had the kettle on the boil. Helen you would love Lauren, she is so like her mum when she was three years old. Her hair is blonde and curly, and she has that mischievous smile that would melt the hardest heart. It was beautiful to see the way Michelle and James embraced, and Lauren who can be somewhat shy at times like this, took to him straight away. He didn't want anything much to eat as he said he was very tired and would like to lie down for awhile. We had some tea and lovely fruit scones that

Michelle had baked at home and brought with her and, after telling us a little about his time in Australia he went for a nap. Well Helen that was four hours ago and still no sound from him. We'll give him a shout when the boys arrive. He's very anxious to meet them it's been so long.

Oh Helen! As I gaze at your picture on my bedside locker, I wonder if you really know I'm talking to you, I believe you do. If I were to believe otherwise I would surely crack up. All I know is I feel your presence all over our home, and I thank God, that even in the vacuum that pervades without you, that He has given me the faith and hope that some day we'll be together again, where no one or anything can ever separate us.

I hear a movement in the other room, I guess James is getting out of bed. This is good as the boys and their families will be here soon. Helen I think it will be a long night, as I'm sure they'll have a mighty lot to catch up on.   Love You.

The Gathering

My beloved wife, talk about a full house. Last evening all the family arrived, and gathered in the sitting room, Tim his wife Irene, their children Michael 14, Seán 12, and Mary 19. Donal and Marie with their son and daughter Pat 12 and Angela 9. Michelle and Liam arrived with their daughters Denise 6 and Lauren 3. We haven't had a night like this since you left us.

After about an hour the lads, Marie and Irene, went across to the Commons Inn for a drink. Michelle and myself stayed to mind the kids. Although some of them are old enough to look after themselves, it was nice Helen to have them together again. My host and socialising skills were put to the test. So much so, that I think that you must having been hovering somewhere in the background, your influence as it used to be guiding me as always. When they returned from the Commons around 9.30 they were in great form, happy to be reunited under the one roof again. Each gathered up their belongings and headed for their own homes, with plans made that all would meet at the Commons for a family lunch today.

All 14 of us sitting at the one table, gossiping, reminiscing, and enjoying the experience. I must say Helen you were deeply missed today, as each had some anecdote to tell.

"If my Mam was here now she would say 'Aren't any of you guys going to say Grace' and then stand up and made sure we all said grace together."

Michelle spoke about the time coming down the Western Road with you.

"Tim remember when she caught you smoking one day on your way down the Western Road, and she admonished you in front of your college friends for having that awful and sinful habit, especially in public. You were 20 then Tim, but I think out of respect for your Mam you never smoked again."

These stories went on and on, one after the other. Helen if you were hovering around I know you surely enjoyed it. Even after 5 years each still feels the pain of your leaving. After lunch and a drink in the bar they called a couple of Taxis, this was 6.30 and the younger ones were getting a bit tired. We said our farewells and they headed to their own homes, with invitations for visits in the near future. It was such a lovely evening that myself and James walked home. James not still being over the jet lag, thanked me for such a lovely day, and went to bed shortly after we arrived home.

I waited for the news on the Tele and I'm really tired after the day.

Before I close my eyes I must say "Thank you Helen" because I know you were with us all through the day. Love and miss you.

Betsy

If there's no one in that wardrobe, What was that noise? Betsy peeped out from under her Barbie quilt. There it is again. It wasn't loud, it was more like a soft thumping and scraping sound. It wasn't easy being 6 and sleeping all alone in your small bedroom. She had heard stories of the Boodie Man, how he could come at night when everyone slept, and take a little girl who had been bold that day away. He would take them to a place where bold girls and boys, would be made to sit up and watch good children eat sweets, ice cream, lollipops, and other goodies, and play with the most wonderful toys. Betsy thought as hard as she could, but could not remember being even the slightest bit bold that day. A song her daddy used to sing to her came into her mind;

"Oh! The wind and the rain brought my daddy back again,

So, go way from the window Boodie Man."

She wished her Daddy were here now. Her mum and dad were gone out to a show and would not be home for at least another two hours. Her Nana was minding herself and her brother. Although she loved her Nan very much, she wondered if in a crisis like this she would be of any help. After all she was old and if she was to hear the noise, she would, more than likely be more frightened than Betsy herself. She might even faint with fear and what would Betsy do then? Someone in the wardrobe, and her Nan in a heap on the floor, no, this was unthinkable. It looked as if she would have to see this through all by herself.

Betsy looked up at the ceiling, the whirls and shapes put up there by her daddy looked different now. The ceiling looked like an overgrown garden full of animals that were gazing at her while she lay there quite still. How is it that things like this only happen when you're all alone and in the dark. Although there was a light over the door it was very dull and small, and was only to show one where the door was situated if one needed to go to the bathroom during the night. Just now it seemed to Betsy, as dull as that light was, it made everything in the room shimmer, and all those shapes move about more.

There, there it is again. The tapping, the scraping, and a swishing sound. Betsy sunk deeper under the quilt and pulled it tightly around her head as if this would ward off any noise, and keep all those ceiling monsters in their place. She heard the door handle turn and a voice, her Nans voice.

"Betsy are you alright love? I thought I heard you moving around."

"Oh Nana, thank goodness you're here. I think I'm having a bad dream. I thought I could hear noises coming from the wardrobe."

" Now, now Betsy dear, there's nothing to be afraid of, there's nothing only your clothes in the wardrobe."

Nana came to her bed and sat her up, put her arms around her to assure her that everything was just fine. Then she thought that she could hear some kind of a noise as well.

Nana put on the bedroom light and said:

"I'll look in the wardrobe now dear, and then we'll see that there's nothing in there only your clothes."

"O.K. But please be careful. I'm not so sure there's no one or nothing in there."

As Nana opened the wardrobe, out jumped one of Betsys most loved toys, Uni the unicorn from the Barbie Swan Lake Ballet. Betsy had forgotten all about him, and that she had put him in the wardrobe for been bold to Barbie that day. He must have been so frightened, all this time shut up inside that wardrobe in the pitch dark. She held him tightly and whispered softly into his ear that she loved him dearly and would never put him out of her sight again.

Just then Betsy remembered her Nan, who, after the fright she got was picking herself up off the floor, and wondering if she was having a bad dream. Had that Unicorn really jumped from the wardrobe on to Betsy's bed? It didn't bear thinking about.

She didn't say anything to Betsy, as her little granddaughter slipped under her quilt again with her two arms around Uni.

"Hush now child, Mammy and Daddy will be home shortly, and you can tell them in the morning all about Uni being locked in the wardrobe and calling to you to be let out."

But Betsy was already fast asleep, and travelling across meadows and streams astride Uni, who had promised Betsy he would never be bold to Barbie again.